Wildlife a
Countryside A

CHAPTER 69

ARRANGEMENT OF SECTIONS

PART I

WILDLIFE

Protection of birds

PART II

NATURE CONSERVATION, COUNTRYSIDE AND NATIONAL PARKS

Nature conservation

Countryside

National Parks

Miscellaneous and supplemental

ELIZABETH II

Wildlife and Countryside Act 1981

1981 CHAPTER 69

An Act to repeal and re-enact with amendments the Protection of Birds Acts 1954 to 1967 and the Conservation of Wild Creatures and Wild Plants Act 1975; to prohibit certain methods of killing or taking wild animals; to amend the law relating to protection of certain mammals; to restrict the introduction of certain animals and plants; to amend the Endangered Species (Import and Export) Act 1976; to amend the law relating to nature conservation, the countryside and National Parks and to make provision with respect to the Countryside Commission; to amend the law relating to public rights of way; and for connected purposes.
[30th October 1981]

BE IT ENACTED by the Queen's most Excellent Majesty, by and with the advice and consent of the Lords Spiritual and Temporal, and Commons, in this present Parliament assembled, and by the authority of the same, as follows:—

PART I

WILDLIFE

Protection of birds

Protection of wild birds, their nests and eggs.

1.—(1) Subject to the provisions of this Part, if any person intentionally—

(*a*) kills, injures or takes any wild bird ;

(*b*) takes, damages or destroys the nest of any wild bird while that nest is in use or being built ; or

(*c*) takes or destroys an egg of any wild bird,

he shall be guilty of an offence.

PART I

(2) Subject to the provisions of this Part, if any person has in his possession or control—

(*a*) any live or dead wild bird or any part of, or anything derived from, such a bird ; or

(*b*) an egg of a wild bird or any part of such an egg,

he shall be guilty of an offence.

(3) A person shall not be guilty of an offence under subsection (2) if he shows that—

(*a*) the bird or egg had not been killed or taken, or had been killed or taken otherwise than in contravention of the relevant provisions ; or

(*b*) the bird, egg or other thing in his possession or control had been sold (whether to him or any other person) otherwise than in contravention of those provisions ;

and in this subsection " the relevant provisions " means the provisions of this Part and of orders made under it and, in the case of a bird or other thing falling within subsection (2)(*a*), the provisions of the Protection of Birds Acts 1954 to 1967 and of orders made under those Acts.

(4) Any person convicted of an offence under subsection (1) or (2) in respect of—

(*a*) a bird included in Schedule 1 or any part of, or anything derived from, such a bird ;

(*b*) the nest of such a bird ; or

(c) an egg of such a bird or any part of such an egg,

shall be liable to a special penalty.

(5) Subject to the provisions of this Part, if any person intentionally—

(*a*) disturbs any wild bird included in Schedule 1 while it is building a nest or is in, on or near a nest containing eggs or young ; or

(*b*) disturbs dependent young of such a bird,

he shall be guilty of an offence and liable to a special penalty.

(6) In this section " wild bird " does not include any bird which is shown to have been bred in captivity.

(7) Any reference in this Part to any bird included in Schedule 1 is a reference to any bird included in Part I and, during the close season for the bird in question, any bird included in Part II of that Schedule.

Exceptions to s. 1.

2.—(1) Subject to the provisions of this section, a person shall not be guilty of an offence under section 1 by reason of the killing or taking of a bird included in Part I of Schedule 2 outside the close season for that bird, or the injuring of such a bird outside that season in the course of an attempt to kill it.

(2) Subject to the provisions of this section, an authorised person shall not be guilty of an offence under section 1 by reason of— PART I

(a) the killing or taking of a bird included in Part II of Schedule 2, or the injuring of such a bird in the course of an attempt to kill it;

(b) the taking, damaging or destruction of a nest of such a bird; or

(c) the taking or destruction of an egg of such a bird.

(3) Subsections (1) and (2) shall not apply in Scotland on Sundays or on Christmas Day; and subsection (1) shall not apply on Sundays in any area of England and Wales which the Secretary of State may by order prescribe for the purposes of that subsection.

(4) In this section and section 1 " close season " means—

(a) in the case of capercaillie and (except in Scotland) woodcock, the period in any year commencing with 1st February and ending with 30th September;

(b) in the case of snipe, the period in any year commencing with 1st February and ending with 11th August;

(c) in the case of wild duck and wild geese in or over any area below high-water mark of ordinary spring tides, the period in any year commencing with 21st February and ending with 31st August;

(d) in any other case, subject to the provisions of this Part, the period in any year commencing with 1st February and ending with 31st August.

(5) The Secretary of State may by order made with respect to the whole or any specified part of Great Britain vary the close season for any wild bird specified in the order.

(6) If it appears to the Secretary of State expedient that any wild birds included in Part II of Schedule 1 or Part I of Schedule 2 should be protected during any period outside the close season for those birds, he may by order made with respect to the whole or any specified part of Great Britain declare any period (which shall not in the case of any order exceed fourteen days) as a period of special protection for those birds; and this section and section 1 shall have effect as if any period of special protection declared under this subsection for any birds formed part of the close season for those birds.

(7) Before making an order under subsection (6) the Secretary of State shall consult a person appearing to him to be a representative of persons interested in the shooting of birds of the kind proposed to be protected by the order.

PART I

Areas of special protection.

3.—(1) The Secretary of State may by order make provision with respect to any area specified in the order providing for all or any of the following matters, that is to say—

(*a*) that any person who, within that area or any part of it specified in the order, at any time or during any period so specified, intentionally—

(i) kills, injures or takes any wild bird or any wild bird so specified ;

(ii) takes, damages or destroys the nest of such a bird while that nest is in use or being built ;

(iii) takes or destroys an egg of such a bird ;

(iv) disturbs such a bird while it is building a nest or is in, on or near a nest containing eggs or young ; or

(v) disturbs dependent young of such a bird,

shall be guilty of an offence under this section ;

(*b*) that any person who, except as may be provided in the order, enters into that area or any part of it specified in the order at any time or during any period so specified shall be guilty of an offence under this section ;

(*c*) that where any offence under this Part, or any such offence under this Part as may be specified in the order, is committed within that area, the offender shall be liable to a special penalty.

(2) An authorised person shall not by virtue of any such order be guilty of an offence by reason of—

(*a*) the killing or taking of a bird included in Part II of Schedule 2, or the injuring of such a bird in the course of an attempt to kill it ;

(*b*) the taking, damaging or destruction of the nest of such a bird ;

(*c*) the taking or destruction of an egg of such a bird ; or

(*d*) the disturbance of such a bird or dependent young of such a bird.

(3) The making of any order under this section with respect to any area shall not affect the exercise by any person of any right vested in him, whether as owner, lessee or occupier of any land in that area or by virtue of a licence or agreement.

(4) Before making any order under this section the Secretary of State shall give particulars of the intended order either by notice in writing to every owner and every occupier of any land included in the area with respect to which the order is to be made or, where the giving of such a notice is in his opinion impracticable, by advertisement in a newspaper circulating in the district in which that area is situated.

PART I

(5) The Secretary of State shall not make an order under this section unless—

(*a*) all the owners and occupiers aforesaid have consented thereto;

(*b*) no objections thereto have been made by any of those owners or occupiers before the expiration of a period of three months from the date of the giving of the notice or the publication of the advertisement; or

(*c*) any such objections so made have been withdrawn.

Exceptions to ss. 1 and 3.

4.—(1) Nothing in section 1 or in any order made under section 3 shall make unlawful—

(*a*) anything done in pursuance of a requirement by the Minister of Agriculture, Fisheries and Food or the Secretary of State under section 98 of the Agriculture Act 1947, or by the Secretary of State under section 39 of the Agriculture (Scotland) Act 1948; 1947 c. 48. 1948 c. 45.

(*b*) anything done under, or in pursuance of an order made under, section 21 or 22 of the Animal Health Act 1981; or 1981 c. 22.

(*c*) except in the case of a wild bird included in Schedule 1 or the nest or egg of such a bird, anything done under, or in pursuance of an order made under, any other provision of the said Act of 1981.

(2) Notwithstanding anything in the provisions of section 1 or any order made under section 3, a person shall not be guilty of an offence by reason of—

(*a*) the taking of any wild bird if he shows that the bird had been disabled otherwise than by his unlawful act and was taken solely for the purpose of tending it and releasing it when no longer disabled;

(*b*) the killing of any wild bird if he shows that the bird had been so seriously disabled otherwise than by his unlawful act that there was no reasonable chance of its recovering; or

(*c*) any act made unlawful by those provisions if he shows that the act was the incidental result of a lawful operation and could not reasonably have been avoided.

(3) Notwithstanding anything in the provisions of section 1 or any order made under section 3, an authorised person shall not be guilty of an offence by reason of the killing or injuring of any wild bird, other than a bird included in Schedule 1, if he shows that his action was necessary for the purpose of—

(*a*) preserving public health or public or air safety;

PART I

(*b*) preventing the spread of disease ; or

(*c*) preventing serious damage to livestock, foodstuffs for livestock, crops, vegetables, fruit, growing timber, or fisheries.

Prohibition of certain methods of killing or taking wild birds.

5.—(1) Subject to the provisions of this Part, if any person—

(*a*) sets in position any of the following articles, being an article which is of such a nature and is so placed as to be calculated to cause bodily injury to any wild bird coming into contact therewith, that is to say, any springe, trap, gin, snare, hook and line, any electrical device for killing, stunning or frightening or any poisonous, poisoned or stupefying substance ;

(*b*) uses for the purpose of killing or taking any wild bird any such article as aforesaid, whether or not of such a nature and so placed as aforesaid, or any net, baited board, bird-lime or substance of a like nature to bird-lime ;

(*c*) uses for the purpose of killing or taking any wild bird—

(i) any bow or crossbow ;

(ii) any explosive other than ammunition for a firearm ;

(iii) any automatic or semi-automatic weapon ;

(iv) any shot-gun of which the barrel has an internal diameter at the muzzle of more than one and three-quarter inches ;

(v) any device for illuminating a target or any sighting device for night shooting ;

(vi) any form of artificial lighting or any mirror or other dazzling device ;

(vii) any gas or smoke not falling within paragraphs (*a*) and (*b*) ; or

(viii) any chemical wetting agent ;

(*d*) uses as a decoy, for the purpose of killing or taking any wild bird, any sound recording or any live bird or other animal whatever which is tethered, or which is secured by means of braces or other similar appliances, or which is blind, maimed or injured ; or

(*e*) uses any mechanically propelled vehicle in immediate pursuit of a wild bird for the purpose of killing or taking that bird,

he shall be guilty of an offence and be liable to a special penalty.

(2) Subject to subsection (3), the Secretary of State may by order, either generally or in relation to any kind of wild bird specified in the order, amend subsection (1) by adding any method of killing or taking wild birds or by omitting any such method which is mentioned in that subsection.

(3) The power conferred by subsection (2) shall not be exerciseable, except for the purpose of complying with an international obligation, in relation to any method of killing or taking wild birds which involves the use of a firearm.

(4) In any proceedings under subsection (1)(*a*) it shall be a defence to show that the article was set in position for the purpose of killing or taking, in the interests of public health, agriculture, forestry, fisheries or nature conservation, any wild animals which could be lawfully killed or taken by those means and that he took all reasonable precautions to prevent injury thereby to wild birds.

(5) Nothing in subsection (1) shall make unlawful—

(*a*) the use of a cage-trap or net by an authorised person for the purpose of taking a bird included in Part II of Schedule 2;

(*b*) the use of nets for the purpose of taking wild duck in a duck decoy which is shown to have been in use immediately before the passing of the Protection of Birds Act 1954; or

1954 c. 30.

(*c*) the use of a cage-trap or net for the purpose of taking any game bird if it is shown that the taking of the bird is solely for the purpose of breeding;

but nothing in this subsection shall make lawful the use of any net for taking birds in flight or the use for taking birds on the ground of any net which is projected or propelled otherwise than by hand.

Sale etc. of live or dead wild birds, eggs etc.

6.—(1) Subject to the provisions of this Part, if any person—

(*a*) sells, offers or exposes for sale, or has in his possession or transports for the purpose of sale, any live wild bird other than a bird included in Part I of Schedule 3, or an egg of a wild bird or any part of such an egg; or

(*b*) publishes or causes to be published any advertisement likely to be understood as conveying that he buys or sells, or intends to buy or sell, any of those things,

he shall be guilty of an offence.

(2) Subject to the provisions of this Part, if any person who is not for the time being registered in accordance with regulations made by the Secretary of State—

(*a*) sells, offers or exposes for sale, or has in his possession or transports for the purpose of sale, any dead wild bird other than a bird included in Part II or III of Schedule 3, or any part of, or anything derived from, such a wild bird; or

PART I

(*b*) publishes or causes to be published any advertisement likely to be understood as conveying that he buys or sells, or intends to buy or sell, any of those things,

he shall be guilty of an offence.

(3) Subject to the provisions of this Part, if any person shows or causes or permits to be shown for the purposes of any competition or in any premises in which a competition is being held—

(*a*) any live wild bird other than a bird included in Part I of Schedule 3 ; or

(*b*) any live bird one of whose parents was such a wild bird,

he shall be guilty of an offence.

(4) Any person convicted of an offence under this section in respect of—

(*a*) a bird included in Schedule 1 or any part of, or anything derived from, such a bird ; or

(*b*) an egg of such bird or any part of such an egg,

shall be liable to a special penalty.

(5) Any reference in this section to any bird included in Part I of Schedule 3 is a reference to any bird included in that Part which was bred in captivity and has been ringed or marked in accordance with regulations made by the Secretary of State ; and regulations so made may make different provision for different birds or different provisions of this section.

(6) Any reference in this section to any bird included in Part II or III of Schedule 3 is a reference to any bird included in Part II and, during the period commencing with 1st September in any year and ending with 28th February of the following year, any bird included in Part III of that Schedule.

(7) The power of the Secretary of State to make regulations under subsection (2) shall include power—

(*a*) to impose requirements as to the carrying out by a person registered in accordance with the regulations of any act which, apart from the registration, would constitute an offence under this section ; and

(*b*) to provide that any contravention of the regulations shall constitute such an offence.

(8) Regulations under subsection (2) shall secure that no person shall become or remain registered—

(*a*) within five years of his having been convicted of an offence under this Part for which a special penalty is provided ; or

(b) within three years of his having been convicted of any other offence under this Part so far as it relates to the protection of birds or other animals or any offence involving their ill-treatment,

no account being taken for this purpose of a conviction which has become spent by virtue of the Rehabilitation of Offenders Act 1974. 1974 c. 53.

(9) Any person authorised in writing by the Secretary of State may, at any reasonable time and (if required to do so) upon producing evidence that he is authorised, enter and inspect any premises where a registered person keeps any wild birds for the purpose of acertaining whether an offence under this section is being, or has been, committed on those premises.

(10) Any person who intentionally obstructs a person acting in the exercise of the power conferred by subsection (9) shall be guilty of an offence.

Registration etc. of certain captive birds.

7.—(1) If any person keeps or has in his possession or under his control any bird included in Schedule 4 which has not been registered and ringed or marked in accordance with regulations made by the Secretary of State, he shall be guilty of an offence and be liable to a special penalty.

(2) The power of the Secretary of State to make regulations under subsection (1) shall include power—

(a) to impose requirements which must be satisfied in relation to a bird included in Schedule 4 before it can be registered in accordance with the regulations; and

(b) to make different provision for different birds or different descriptions of birds.

(3) If any person keeps or has in his possession or under his control any bird included in Schedule 4—

(a) within five years of his having been convicted of an offence under this Part for which a special penalty is provided; or

(b) within three years of his having been convicted of any other offence under this Part so far as it relates to the protection of birds or other animals or any offence involving their ill-treatment,

he shall be guilty of an offence.

(4) If any person knowingly disposes of or offers to dispose of any bird included in Schedule 4 to any person—

(a) within five years of that person's having been convicted of such an offence as is mentioned in paragraph (a) of subsection (3); or

PART I

(*b*) within three years of that person's having been convicted of such an offence as is mentioned in paragraph (*b*) of that subsection,

he shall be guilty of an offence.

1974 c. 53.

(5) No account shall be taken for the purposes of subsections (3) and (4) of any conviction which has become spent for the purpose of the Rehabilitation of Offenders Act 1974.

(6) Any person authorised in writing by the Secretary of State may, at any reasonable time and (if required to do so) upon producing evidence that he is authorised, enter and inspect any premises where any birds included in Schedule 4 are kept for the purpose of ascertaining whether an offence under this section is being, or has been, committed on those premises.

(7) Any person who intentionally obstructs a person acting in the exercise of the power conferred by subsection (6) shall be guilty of an offence.

Protection of captive birds.

8.—(1) If any person keeps or confines any bird whatever in any cage or other receptacle which is not sufficient in height, length or breadth to permit the bird to stretch its wings freely, he shall be guilty of an offence and be liable to a special penalty.

(2) Subsection (1) does not apply to poultry, or to the keeping or confining of any bird—

(*a*) while that bird is in the course of conveyance, by whatever means;

(*b*) while that bird is being shown for the purposes of any public exhibition or competition if the time during which the bird is kept or confined for those purposes does not in the aggregate exceed 72 hours; or

(*c*) while that bird is undergoing examination or treatment by a veterinary surgeon or veterinary practitioner.

(3) Every person who—

(*a*) promotes, arranges, conducts, assists in, receives money for, or takes part in, any event whatever at or in the course of which captive birds are liberated by hand or by any other means whatever for the purpose of being shot immediately after their liberation; or

(*b*) being the owner or occupier of any land, permits that land to be used for the purposes of such an event,

shall be guilty of an offence and be liable to a special penalty.

Protection of other animals

Protection of certain wild animals.

9.—(1) Subject to the provisions of this Part, if any person intentionally kills, injures or takes any wild animal included in Schedule 5, he shall be guilty of an offence.

(2) Subject to the provisions of this Part, if any person has in his possession or control any live or dead wild animal included in Schedule 5 or any part of, or anything derived from, such an animal, he shall be guilty of an offence.

(3) A person shall not be guilty of an offence under subsection (2) if he shows that—

(*a*) the animal had not been killed or taken, or had been killed or taken otherwise than in contravention of the relevant provisions ; or

(*b*) the animal or other thing in his possession or control had been sold (whether to him or any other person) otherwise than in contravention of those provisions ;

and in this subsection " the relevant provisions " means the provisions of this Part and of the Conservation of Wild Creatures and Wild Plants Act 1975. 1975 c. 48.

(4) Subject to the provisions of this Part, if any person intentionally—

(*a*) damages or destroys, or obstructs access to, any structure or place which any wild animal included in Schedule 5 uses for shelter or protection ; or

(*b*) disturbs any such animal while it is occupying a structure or place which it uses for that purpose,

he shall be guilty of an offence.

(5) Subject to the provisions of this Part, if any person—

(*a*) sells, offers or exposes for sale, or has in his possession or transports for the purpose of sale, any live or dead wild animal included in Schedule 5, or any part of, or anything derived from, such an animal ; or

(*b*) publishes or causes to be published any advertisement likely to be understood as conveying that he buys or sells, or intends to buy or sell, any of those things,

he shall be guilty of an offence.

(6) In any proceedings for an offence under subsection (1), (2) or (5)(*a*), the animal in question shall be presumed to have been a wild animal unless the contrary is shown.

PART I

Exceptions to s. 9.

10. (1) Nothing in section 9 shall make unlawful—

(*a*) anything done in pursuance of a requirement by the Minister of Agriculture, Fisheries and Food or the Secretary of State under section 98 of the Agriculture Act 1947, or by the Secretary of State under section 39 of the Agriculture (Scotland) Act 1948; or

1947 c. 48.
1948 c. 45.

(*b*) anything done under, or in pursuance of an order made under, the Animal Health Act 1981.

1981 c. 22.

(2) Nothing in subsection (4) of section 9 shall make unlawful anything done within a dwelling-house.

(3) Notwithstanding anything in section 9, a person shall not be guilty of an offence by reason of—

(*a*) the taking of any such animal if he shows that the animal had been disabled otherwise than by his unlawful act and was taken solely for the purpose of tending it and releasing it when no longer disabled;

(*b*) the killing of any such animal if he shows that the animal had been so seriously disabled otherwise than by his unlawful act that there was no reasonable chance of its recovering; or

(*c*) any act made unlawful by that section if he shows that the act was the incidental result of a lawful operation and could not reasonably have been avoided.

(4) Notwithstanding anything in section 9, an authorised person shall not be guilty of an offence by reason of the killing or injuring of a wild animal included in Schedule 5 if he shows that his action was necessary for the purpose of preventing serious damage to livestock, foodstuffs for livestock, crops, vegetables, fruit, growing timber or any other form of property or to fisheries.

(5) A person shall not be entitled to rely on the defence provided by subsection (2) or (3)(*c*) as respects anything done in relation to a bat otherwise than in the living area of a dwelling house unless he had notified the Nature Conservancy Council of the proposed action or operation and allowed them a reasonable time to advise him as to whether it should be carried out and, if so, the method to be used.

(6) An authorised person shall not be entitled to rely on the defence provided by subsection (4) as respects any action taken at any time if it had become apparent, before that time, that that action would prove necessary for the purpose mentioned in that subsection and either—

(*a*) a licence under section 16 authorising that action had not been applied for as soon as reasonably practicable after that fact had become apparent; or

(*b*) an application for such a licence had been determined.

Prohibition of certain methods of killing or taking wild animals.

11.—(1) Subject to the provisions of this Part, if any person—

(*a*) sets in position any self-locking snare which is of such a nature and so placed as to be calculated to cause bodily injury to any wild animal coming into contact therewith;

(*b*) uses for the purpose of killing or taking any wild animal any self-locking snare, whether or not of such a nature or so placed as aforesaid, any bow or cross-bow or any explosive other than ammunition for a firearm; or

(*c*) uses as a decoy, for the purpose of killing or taking any wild animal, any live mammal or bird whatever,

he shall be guilty of an offence.

(2) Subject to the provisions of this Part, if any person—

(*a*) sets in position any of the following articles, being an article which is of such a nature and so placed as to be calculated to cause bodily injury to any wild animal included in Schedule 6 which comes into contact there-with, that is to say, any trap or snare, any electrical device for killing or stunning or any poisonous, poisoned or stupefying substance;

(*b*) uses for the purpose of killing or taking any such wild animal any such article as aforesaid, whether or not of such a nature and so placed as aforesaid, or any net;

(*c*) uses for the purpose of killing or taking any such wild animal—

(i) any automatic or semi-automatic weapon;

(ii) any device for illuminating a target or sighting device for night shooting;

(iii) any form of artificial light or any mirror or other dazzling device; or

(iv) any gas or smoke not falling within paragraphs (*a*) and (*b*);

(*d*) uses as a decoy, for the purpose of killing or taking any such wild animal, any sound recording; or

(*e*) uses any mechanically propelled vehicle in immediate pursuit of any such wild animal for the purpose of driving, killing or taking that animal,

he shall be guilty of an offence.

(3) Subject to the provisions of this Part, if any person—

(*a*) sets in position any snare which is of such a nature and so placed as to be calculated to cause bodily injury to any wild animal coming into contact therewith; and

PART I

(b) while the snare remains in position fails, without reasonable excuse, to inspect it, or cause it to be inspected, at least once every day,

he shall be guilty of an offence.

(4) The Secretary of State may, for the purpose of complying with an international obligation, by order, either generally or in relation to any kind of wild animal specified in the order, amend subsection (1) or (2) by adding any method of killing or taking wild animals or by omitting any such method as is mentioned in that subsection.

(5) In any proceedings for an offence under subsection (1)(*b*) or (*c*) or (2)(*b*), (*c*), (*d*) or (*e*), the animal in question shall be presumed to have been a wild animal unless the contrary is shown.

(6) In any proceedings for an offence under subsection (2)(*a*) it shall be a defence to show that the article was set in position by the accused for the purpose of killing or taking, in the interests of public health, agriculture, forestry, fisheries or nature conservation, any wild animals which could be lawfully killed or taken by those means and that he took all reasonable precautions to prevent injury thereby to any wild animals included in Schedule 6.

Protection of certain mammals.

12. Schedule 7, which amends the law relating to the protection of certain mammals, shall have effect.

Protection of plants

Protection of wild plants.

13.—(1) Subject to the provisions of this Part, if any person—

(*a*) intentionally picks, uproots or destroys any wild plant included in Schedule 8 ; or

(*b*) not being an authorised person, intentionally uproots any wild plant not included in that Schedule,

he shall be guilty of an offence.

(2) Subject to the provisions of this Part, if any person—

(*a*) sells, offers or exposes for sale, or has in his possession or transports for the purpose of sale, any live or dead wild plant included in Schedule 8, or any part of, or anything derived from, such a plant ; or

(*b*) publishes or causes to be published any advertisement likely to be understood as conveying that he buys or sells, or intends to buy or sell, any of those things,

he shall be guilty of an offence.

(3) Notwithstanding anything in subsection (1), a person shall not be guilty of an offence by reason of any act made unlawful by that subsection if he shows that the act was an incidental result of a lawful operation and could not reasonably have been avoided. PART I

(4) In any proceedings for an offence under subsection (2)(*a*), the plant in question shall be presumed to have been a wild plant unless the contrary is shown.

Miscellaneous

14.—(1) Subject to the provisions of this Part, if any person releases or allows to escape into the wild any animal which— **Introduction of new species etc.**

(*a*) is of a kind which is not ordinarily resident in and is not a regular visitor to Great Britain in a wild state ; or

(*b*) is included in Part I of Schedule 9,

he shall be guilty of an offence.

(2) Subject to the provisions of this Part, if any person plants or otherwise causes to grow in the wild any plant which is included in Part II of Schedule 9, he shall be guilty of an offence.

(3) Subject to subsection (4), it shall be a defence to a charge of committing an offence under subsection (1) or (2) to prove that the accused took all reasonable steps and exercised all due diligence to avoid committing the offence.

(4) Where the defence provided by subsection (3) involves an allegation that the commission of the offence was due to the act or default of another person, the person charged shall not, without leave of the court, be entitled to rely on the defence unless, within a period ending seven clear days before the hearing, he has served on the prosecutor a notice giving such information identifying or assisting in the identification of the other person as was then in his possession.

(5) Any person authorised in writing by the Secretary of State may, at any reasonable time and (if required to do so) upon producing evidence that he is authorised, enter any land for the purpose of ascertaining whether an offence under subsection (1) or (2) is being, or has been, committed on that land ; but nothing in this subsection shall authorise any person to enter a dwelling.

(6) Any person who intentionally obstructs a person acting in the exercise of the power conferred by subsection (5) shall be guilty of an offence.

PART I

Endangered species (import and export).

1976 c. 72.

15.—(1) The Endangered Species (Import and Export) Act 1976 shall have effect subject to the amendments provided for in Schedule 10; and in that Schedule "the 1976 Act" means that Act.

(2) The functions of the Nature Conservancy Council shall include power to advise or assist—

(*a*) any constable;

(*b*) any officer commissioned or other person appointed or authorised by the Commissioners of Customs and Excise to exercise any function conferred on the Commissioners by the said Act of 1976; or

(*c*) any person duly authorised by the Secretary of State under section 7(3) of that Act,

in, or in connection with, the enforcement of that Act or any order made under it.

Supplemental

Power to grant licences.

16.—(1) Sections 1, 5, 6(3), 7 and 8 and orders under section 3 do not apply to anything done—

(*a*) for scientific or educational purposes;

(*b*) for the purpose of ringing or marking, or examining any ring or mark on, wild birds;

(*c*) for the purpose of conserving wild birds;

(*d*) for the purpose of protecting any collection of wild birds;

(*e*) for the purposes of falconry or aviculture;

(*f*) for the purposes of any public exhibition or competition;

(*g*) for the purposes of taxidermy;

(*h*) for the purpose of photography;

(*i*) for the purposes of preserving public health or public or air safety;

(*j*) for the purpose of preventing the spread of disease; or

(*k*) for the purposes of preventing serious damage to livestock, foodstuffs for livestock, crops, vegetables, fruit, growing timber or fisheries,

if it is done under and in accordance with the terms of a licence granted by the appropriate authority.

(2) Section 1 and orders under section 3 do not apply to anything done for the purpose of providing food for human consumption in relation to—

(*a*) a gannet on the island of Sula Sgeir; or

(*b*) a gull's egg or, at any time before 15th April in any year, a lapwing's egg,

if it is done under and in accordance with the terms of a licence granted by the appropriate authority.

(3) Sections 9(1), (2) and (4), 11(1) and (2) and 13(1) do not apply to anything done—

(*a*) for scientific or educational purposes;

(*b*) for the purpose of ringing or marking, or examining any ring or mark on, wild animals;

(*c*) for the purpose of conserving wild animals or wild plants or introducing them to particular areas;

(*d*) for the purpose of protecting any zoological or botanical collection;

(*e*) for the purpose of photography;

(*f*) for the purpose of preserving public health or public safety;

(*g*) for the purpose of preventing the spread of disease; or

(*h*) for the purpose of preventing serious damage to livestock, foodstuffs for livestock, crops, vegetables, fruit, growing timber or any other form of property or to fisheries,

if it is done under and in accordance with the terms of a licence granted by the appropriate authority.

(4) The following provisions, namely—

(*a*) section 6(1) and (2);

(*b*) sections 9(5) and 13(2); and

(*c*) section 14,

do not apply to anything done under and in accordance with the terms of a licence granted by the appropriate authority.

(5) Subject to subsection (6), a licence under the foregoing provisions of this section—

(*a*) may be, to any degree, general or specific;

(*b*) may be granted either to persons of a class or to a particular person;

(*c*) may be subject to compliance with any specified conditions;

(*d*) may be modified or revoked at any time by the appropriate authority; and

(*e*) subject to paragraph (*d*), shall be valid for the period stated in the licence;

and the appropriate authority may charge therefor such reasonable sum (if any) as they may determine.

PART I

(6) A licence under subsection (1), (2) or (3) which authorises any person to kill wild birds or wild animals—

(*a*) shall specify the area within which, and the methods by which the wild birds or wild animals may be killed; and

(*b*) subject to subsection (5)(*d*), shall be valid for the period, not exceeding two years, stated in the licence.

(7) It shall be a defence in proceedings for an offence under section 8(*b*) of the Protection of Animals Act 1911 or section 7(*b*) of the Protection of Animals (Scotland) Act 1912 (which restrict the placing on land of poison and poisonous substances) to show that—

1911 c. 27.
1912 c. 14.

(*a*) the act alleged to constitute the offence was done under and in accordance with the terms of a licence issued under subsection (1) or (3); and

(*b*) any conditions specified in the licence were complied with.

(8) For the purposes of a licence granted under the foregoing provisions of this section, the definition of a class of persons may be framed by reference to any circumstances whatever including, in particular, their being authorised by any other person.

(9) In this section " the appropriate authority " means—

(*a*) in the case of a licence under paragraph (*a*), (*b*) or (*c*) of subsection (1), either the Secretary of State after consultation with whichever one of the advisory bodies he considers is best able to advise him as to whether the licence should be granted, or the Nature Conservancy Council;

(*b*) in the case of a licence under any of paragraphs (*d*) to (*g*) of subsection (1), subsection (2) or paragraph (*a*) or (*b*) of subsection (4), the Secretary of State after such consultation as aforesaid;

(*c*) in the case of a licence under paragraph (*h*) of subsection (1) or any of paragraphs (*a*) to (*e*) of subsection (3), the Nature Conservancy Council;

(*d*) in the case of a licence under paragraph (*i*), (*j*) or (*k*) of subsection (1) or paragraph (*f*), (*g*) or (*h*) of subsection (3) or a licence under paragraph (*c*) of subsection (4) which authorises anything to be done in relation to fish or shellfish, the agriculture Minister; and

(*e*) in the case of any other licence under paragraph (*c*) of subsection (4), the Secretary of State.

(10) The agriculture Minister—

(*a*) shall from time to time consult with the Nature Conservancy Council as to the exercise of his functions under this section ; and

(*b*) shall not grant a licence of any description unless he has been advised by the Council as to the circumstances in which, in their opinion, licences of that description should be granted.

False statements made for obtaining registration or licence etc.

17. A person who, for the purposes of obtaining, whether for himself or another, a registration in accordance with regulations made under section 6(2) or 7(1) or the grant of a licence under section 16—

(*a*) makes a statement or representation, or furnishes a document or information, which he knows to be false in a material particular ; or

(*b*) recklessly makes a statement or representation, or furnishes a document or information, which is false in a material particular,

shall be guilty of an offence.

Attempts to commit offences etc.

18.—(1) Any person who attempts to commit an offence under the foregoing provisions of this Part shall be guilty of an offence and shall be punishable in like manner as for the said offence.

(2) Any person who for the purposes of committing an offence under the foregoing provisions of this Part, has in his possession anything capable of being used for committing the offence shall be guilty of an offence and shall be punishable in like manner as for the said offence.

Enforcement.

19.—(1) If a constable suspects with reasonable cause that any person is committing or has committed an offence under this Part, the constable may without warrant—

(*a*) stop and search that person if the constable suspects with reasonable cause that evidence of the commission of the offence is to be found on that person ;

(*b*) search or examine any thing which that person may then be using or have in his possession if the constable suspects with reasonable cause that evidence of the commission of the offence is to be found on that thing ;

(*c*) arrest that person if he fails to give his name and address to the constable's satisfaction ;

PART I

(*d*) seize and detain for the purposes of proceedings under this Part any thing which may be evidence of the commission of the offence or may be liable to be forfeited under section 21.

(2) If a constable suspects with reasonable cause that any person is committing an offence under this Part, he may, for the purpose of exercising the powers conferred by subsection (1), enter any land other than a dwelling-house.

(3) If a justice of the peace is satisfied by information on oath that there are reasonable grounds for suspecting that—

(*a*) an offence under section 1, 3, 5, 7 or 8 in respect of which this Part or any order made under it provides for a special penalty ; or

(*b*) an offence under section 6, 9, 11(1) or (2), 13 or 14,

has been committed and that evidence of the offence may be found on any premises, he may grant a warrant to any constable (with or without other persons) to enter upon and search those premises for the purpose of obtaining that evidence.

In the application of this subsection to Scotland, the reference to a justice of the peace includes a reference to the sheriff.

Summary prosecutions.

20.—(1) This section applies to—

(*a*) any offence under section 1(1) or 3(1) involving the killing or taking of any wild bird or the taking of an egg of such a bird ;

(*b*) any offence under section 9(1) involving the killing or taking of any wild animal ; and

(*c*) any offence under section 13(1) involving the picking uprooting or destruction of any wild plant.

(2) Summary proceedings for an offence to which this section applies may be brought within a period of six months from the date on which evidence sufficient in the opinion of the prosecutor to warrant the proceedings came to his knowledge ; but no such proceedings shall be brought by virtue of this section more than two years after the commission of the offence.

(3) For the purpose of this section a certificate signed by or on behalf of the prosecutor and stating the date on which such evidence as aforesaid came to his knowledge shall be conclusive evidence of that fact ; and a certificate stating that matter and purporting to be so signed shall be deemed to be so signed unless the contrary is proved.

PART I

Penalties, forfeitures etc.

21.—(1) Subject to subsection (5), a person guilty of an offence under section 1, 3, 5, 6, 7 or 8 shall be liable on summary conviction—

(*a*) in a case where this Part or any order made under it provides that he shall be liable to a special penalty, to a fine not exceeding £1,000 ;

(*b*) in any other case, to a fine not exceeding £200.

(2) Subject to subsection (5), a person guilty of an offence under section 9 or 11(1) or (2) shall be liable on summary conviction to a fine not exceeding £1,000.

(3) Subject to subsection (5), a person guilty of an offence under section 11(3), 13 or 17 shall be liable on summary conviction to a fine not exceeding £500.

(4) A person guilty of an offence under section 14 shall be liable—

(*a*) on summary conviction, to a fine not exceeding the statutory maximum ;

(*b*) on conviction on indictment, to a fine.

(5) Where an offence to which subsection (1), (2) or (3) applies was committed in respect of more than one bird, nest, egg, other animal, plant or other thing, the maximum fine which may be imposed under that subsection shall be determined as if the person convicted had been convicted of a separate offence in respect of each bird, nest, egg, animal, plant or thing.

(6) The court by which any person is convicted of an offence under this Part—

(*a*) shall order the forfeiture of any bird, nest, egg, other animal, plant or other thing in respect of which the offence was committed ; and

(*b*) may order the forfeiture of any vehicle, animal, weapon or other thing which was used to commit the offence and, in the case of an offence under section 14, any animal or plant which is of the same kind as that in respect of which the offence was committed and was found in his possession.

(7) Any offence under this Part shall, for the purpose of conferring jurisdiction, be deemed to have been committed in any place where the offender is found or to which he is first brought after the commission of the offence.

Power to vary Schedules.

22.—(1) The Secretary of State may by order, either generally or with respect to particular provisions of this Part, particular areas of Great Britain or particular times of the year, add any bird to, or remove any bird from, any of or any Part of Schedules 1 to 4.

PART I

(2) An order under subsection (1) adding any bird to Part II of Schedule 1 or Part I of Schedule 2 may prescribe a close season in the case of that bird for the purposes of sections 1 and 2; and any close season so prescribed shall commence on a date not later than 21st February and end on a date not earlier than 31st August.

(3) The Secretary of State may, on a representation made to him by the Nature Conservancy Council, by order, either generally or with respect to particular provisions of this Part, particular areas of Great Britain or particular times of the year—

(*a*) add to Schedule 5 or Schedule 8 any animal or plant which, in his opinion, is in danger of extinction in Great Britain or is likely to become so endangered unless conservation measures are taken; and

(*b*) remove from Schedule 5 or Schedule 8 any animal or plant which, in his opinion, is no longer so endangered or likely to become so endangered.

(4) The Secretary of State may, for the purpose of complying with an international obligation, by order, either generally or with respect to particular provisions of this Part or particular times of the year—

(*a*) add any animals to, or remove any animals from, Schedule 5 or Schedule 6; and

(*b*) add any plants to, or remove any plants from, Schedule 8.

(5) The Secretary of State may by order, either generally or with respect to particular areas of Great Britain—

(*a*) add any animals to, or remove any animals from, Part I of Schedule 9; and

(*b*) add any plants to, or remove any plants from, Part II of that Schedule.

Advisory bodies and their functions.

23.—(1) The Secretary of State may—

(*a*) establish any body or bodies, consisting in each case of such members as he may from time to time appoint;

(*b*) assign to any body or bodies the duty referred to in subsection (4).

(2) Without prejudice to his power under subsection (1), the Secretary of State shall, as soon as practicable after the commencement date,—

(*a*) establish at least one body under paragraph (*a*) of subsection (1); or

(*b*) assign to at least one body, under paragraph (*b*) of that subsection, the duty referred to in subsection (4).

PART I

(3) A reference in this Part to an advisory body is a reference to a body which is established under subsection (1) or to which the duty there referred to is assigned under that subsection.

(4) It shall be the duty of an advisory body to advise the Secretary of State on any question which he may refer to it or on which it considers it should offer its advice—

(*a*) in connection with the administration of this Part; or

(*b*) otherwise in connection with the protection of birds or other animals or plants.

(5) In so far as it does not have power to do so apart from this subsection, an advisory body may publish reports relating to the performance by it of its duty under subsection (4).

(6) Before appointing a person to be a member of an advisory body established under subsection (1)(*a*), the Secretary of State shall consult such persons or bodies as he thinks fit.

(7) The Secretary of State may, out of moneys provided by Parliament and to such an extent as may be approved by the Treasury, defray or contribute towards the expenses of an advisory body established under subsection (1)(*a*).

Functions of Nature Conservancy Council.

24.—(1) The Nature Conservancy Council may at any time and shall five years after the passing of this Act and every five years thereafter, review Schedules 5 and 8 and advise the Secretary of State whether, in their opinion,—

(*a*) any animal should be added to, or removed from, Schedule 5;

(*b*) any plant should be added to, or removed from, Schedule 8.

(2) Advice may be given under subsection (1) either generally or with respect to particular provisions of this Part, particular areas of Great Britain or particular times of the year; and any advice so given shall be accompanied by a statement of the reasons which led the Council to give that advice.

(3) The Council shall include any advice so given and the statement accompanying it in the annual report submitted by them to the Secretary of State under paragraph 17 of Schedule 3 to the Nature Conservancy Council Act 1973. **1973 c. 54.**

(4) The functions of the Council shall include power to advise or assist—

(*a*) any constable;

(*b*) any proper officer of a local authority; or

(*c*) any person duly authorised by the Secretary of State under section 6(9), 7(6) or 14(5),

in, or in connection with, the enforcement of the provisions of this Part or any order or regulations made under it.

PART I

Functions of local authorities.

25.—(1) Every local authority shall take such steps as they consider expedient for bringing to the attention of the public and of schoolchildren in particular the effect of—

(*a*) the provisions of this Part ; and

(*b*) any order made under this Part affecting the whole or any part of their area.

(2) A local authority in England and Wales may institute proceedings for any offence under this Part or any order made under it which is committed within their area.

Regulations, orders, notices etc.

26.—(1) Any power to make regulations or orders under this Part shall be exercisable by statutory instrument.

(2) A statutory instrument containing regulations under this Part, or an order under a provision of this Part other than sections 2(6), 3, 5 and 11, shall be subject to annulment in pursuance of a resolution of either House of Parliament.

(3) No order under section 5 or 11 shall be made unless a draft of the order has been laid before and approved by a resolution of each House of Parliament.

(4) Before making any order under this Part, the Secretary of State—

(*a*) except in the case of an order under section 2(6), shall give to any local authority affected and, except in the case of an order under section 3, any other person affected, by such means as he may think appropriate, an opportunity to submit objections or representations with respect to the subject matter of the order ;

(*b*) except in the case of an order under section 22(3), shall consult with whichever one of the advisory bodies he considers is best able to advise him as to whether the order should be made ; and

(*c*) may, if he thinks fit, cause a public inquiry to be held.

(5) Notice of the making of an order under this Part shall be published by the Secretary of State—

(*a*) if the order relates in whole or in part to England and Wales, in the London Gazette ; and

(*b*) if the order relates in whole or in part to Scotland, in the Edinburgh Gazette.

(6) The Secretary of State shall give consideration to any proposals for the making by him of an order under this Part with respect to any area which may be submitted to him by a local authority whose area includes that area.

PART I

27.—(1) In this Part, unless the context otherwise requires— Interpretation of Part I.

" advertisement " includes a catalogue, a circular and a price list ;

" advisory body " has the meaning given by section 23 ;

" agriculture Minister " means the Minister of Agriculture, Fisheries and Food or the Secretary of State ;

" authorised person " means—

(*a*) the owner or occupier, or any person authorised by the owner or occupier, of the land on which the action authorised is taken ;

(*b*) any person authorised in writing by the local authority for the area within which the action authorised is taken ;

(*c*) as respects anything done in relation to wild birds, any person authorised in writing by any of the following bodies, that is to say, the Nature Conservancy Council, a water authority or any other statutory water undertakers, a district board for a fishery district within the meaning of the Salmon Fisheries (Scotland) Act 1862 or a local fisheries committee constituted under the Sea Fisheries Regulation Act 1966 ;

1862 c. 97.
1966 c. 38.

so, however, that the authorisation of any person for the purposes of this definition shall not confer any right of entry upon any land ;

" automatic weapon " and " semi-automatic weapon " do not include any weapon the magazine of which is incapable of holding more than two rounds ;

" aviculture " means the breeding and rearing of birds in captivity ;

" destroy ", in relation to an egg, includes doing anything to the egg which is calculated to prevent it from hatching, and " destruction " shall be construed accordingly ;

" domestic duck " means any domestic form of duck ;

" domestic goose " means any domestic form of goose ;

" firearm " has the same meaning as in the Firearms Act 1968 ; 1968 c. 27.

" game bird " means any pheasant, partridge, grouse (or moor game), black (or heath) game or ptarmigan ;

" livestock " includes any animal which is kept—

(*a*) for the provision of food, wool, skins or fur ;

(*b*) for the purpose of its use in the carrying on of any agricultural activity ; or

(*c*) for the provision or improvement of shooting or fishing ;

PART I

" local authority " means—

(*a*) in relation to England and Wales, a county, district or London borough council and the Greater London Council ;

(*b*) in relation to Scotland, a regional, islands or district council ;

" occupier ", in relation to any land other than the foreshore, includes any person having any right of hunting, shooting, fishing or taking game or fish ;

" pick ", in relation to a plant, means gather or pluck any part of the plant without uprooting it ;

" poultry " means domestic fowls, geese, ducks, guinea-fowls, pigeons and quails, and turkeys ;

" sale " includes hire, barter and exchange and cognate expressions shall be construed accordingly ;

" uproot ", in relation to a plant, means dig up or otherwise remove the plant from the land on which it is growing ;

" vehicle " includes aircraft, hovercraft and boat ;

" water authority ", in relation to Scotland, has the same meaning as in the Water (Scotland) Act 1980 ;

1980 c. 45.

" wild animal " means any animal (other than a bird) which is or (before it was killed or taken) was living wild ;

" wild bird " means any bird of a kind which is ordinarily resident in or is a visitor to Great Britain in a wild state but does not include poultry or, except in sections 5 and 16, any game bird ;

" wild plant " means any plant which is or (before it was picked, uprooted or destroyed) was growing wild and is of a kind which ordinarily grows in Great Britain in a wild state.

(2) A bird shall not be treated as bred in captivity for the purposes of this Part unless its parents were lawfully in captivity when the egg was laid.

(3) Any reference in this Part to an animal of any kind includes, unless the context otherwise requires, a reference to an egg, larva, pupa, or other immature stage of an animal of that kind.

(4) This Part shall apply to the Isles of Scilly as if the Isles were a county and as if the Council of the Isles were a county council.

(5) This Part extends to the territorial waters adjacent to Great Britain, and for the purposes of this Part any part of Great Britain which is bounded by territorial waters shall be taken to include the territorial waters adjacent to that part.

PART II

NATURE CONSERVATION, COUNTRYSIDE AND NATIONAL PARKS

Nature conservation

28.—(1) Where the Nature Conservancy Council are of the opinion that any area of land is of special interest by reason of any of its flora, fauna, or geological or physiographical features, it shall be the duty of the Council to notify that fact— Areas of special scientific interest.

(*a*) to the local planning authority in whose area the land is situated ;

(*b*) to every owner and occupier of any of that land ; and

(*c*) to the Secretary of State.

(2) Before giving a notification under subsection (1), the Council shall give notice to the persons mentioned in that subsection—

(*a*) setting out the proposed notification ; and

(*b*) specifying the time (not being less than three months from the date of the giving of the notice) within which and the manner in which, representations or objections with respect thereto may be made,

and shall consider any representation or objections duly made.

(3) If, after reasonable inquiry has been made, the Council are satisfied that it is not practicable to ascertain the name or address of an owner or occupier of any land a notification or notice required to be served on him may be served by addressing it to him by the description " owner " or " occupier " of the land (describing it) and by affixing it to some conspicuous object or objects on the land.

(4) A notification under subsection (1)(*b*) shall specify—

(*a*) the flora, fauna, or geological or physiographical features by reason of which the land is of special interest ; and

(*b*) any operations appearing to the Council to be likely to damage that flora or fauna or those features.

(5) The owner or occupier of any land which has been notified under subsection (1)(*b*) shall not carry out, or cause or permit to be carried out, on that land any operation specified in the notification unless—

(*a*) one of them has, after the commencement date, given the Council written notice of a proposal to carry out the operation specifying its nature and the land on which it is proposed to carry it out ; and

(*b*) one of the conditions specified in subsection (6) is fulfilled.

PART II

(6) The said conditions are—

(*a*) that the operation is carried out with the Council's written consent;

(*b*) that the operation is carried out in accordance with the terms of an agreement under section 16 of the 1949 Act or section 15 of the 1968 Act; and

(*c*) that three months have expired from the giving of the notice under subsection (5).

(7) A person who, without reasonable excuse, contravenes subsection (5) shall be liable on summary conviction to a fine not exceeding £500.

(8) It is a reasonable excuse in any event for a person to carry out an operation if—

(*a*) the operation was authorised by a planning permission granted on an application under Part III of the Town and Country Planning Act 1971 or Part III of the Town and Country Planning (Scotland) Act 1972; or

1971 c. 78.
1972 c. 52.

(*b*) the operation was an emergency operation particulars of which (including details of the emergency) were notified to the Council as soon as practicable after the commencement of the operation.

(9) The Council shall have power to enforce the provisions of this section; but nothing in this subsection shall be construed as authorising the Council to institute proceedings in Scotland for an offence.

(10) Proceedings in England and Wales for an offence under subsection (7) shall not, without the consent of the Director of Public Prosecutions, be taken by a person other than the Council.

(11) A notification under subsection (1)(*b*) of land in England and Wales shall be a local land charge.

(12) A notification under subsection (1)(*b*) of land in Scotland shall be registered either—

(*a*) in a case where the land is registered in that Register, in the Land Register of Scotland; or

(*b*) in any other case, in the appropriate Division of the General Register of Sasines.

(13) Section 23 of the 1949 Act (which is superseded by this section) shall cease to have effect; but any notification given under that section shall have effect as if given under subsection (1)(*a*).

(14) Subsection (2) shall not apply in relation to a notification of any land under subsection (1)(*b*) where a notification of that land under the said section 23 has effect as if given under subsection (1)(*a*).

PART II

Special protection for certain areas of special scientific interest.

29.—(1) Where it appears to the Secretary of State expedient to do so—

(*a*) in the case of any land to which this paragraph applies, for the purpose of securing the survival in Great Britain of any kind of animal or plant or of complying with an international obligation; or

(*b*) in the case of any land to which this paragraph applies, for the purpose of conserving any of its flora, fauna, or geological or physiographical features,

he may, after consultation with the Nature Conservancy Council, by order apply subsection (3) to that land; and the provisions of Schedule 11 shall have effect as to the making, confirmation and coming into operation of orders under this section.

An order made under this section may be amended or revoked by a subsequent order so made.

(2) Paragraphs (*a*) and (*b*) of subsection (1) apply to any land which in the opinion of the Secretary of State is—

(*a*) of special interest; and

(*b*) in the case of paragraph (*b*) of that subsection, of national importance,

by reason of any of its flora, fauna, or geological or physiographical features.

(3) Subject to subsection (4), no person shall carry out on any land to which this subsection applies any operation which—

(*a*) appears to the Secretary of State to be likely to destroy or damage the flora, fauna, or geological or physiographical features by reason of which the land is land to which paragraph (*a*) or, as the case may be, paragraph (*b*) of subsection (1) applies; and

(*b*) is specified in the order applying this subsection to the land.

(4) Subsection (3) shall not apply in relation to any operation carried out, or caused or permitted to be carried out, by the owner or occupier of the land if—

(*a*) one of them has, after the commencement date, given the Council notice of a proposal to carry out the operation, specifying its nature and the land on which it is proposed to carry it out; and

(*b*) one of the conditions specified in subsection (5) is fulfilled.

(5) The said conditions are—

(*a*) that the operation is carried out with the Council's written consent;

PART II

(*b*) that the operation is carried out in accordance with the terms of an agreement under section 16 of the 1949 Act or section 15 of the 1968 Act ; and

(*c*) subject to subsections (6) and (7), that three months have expired from the giving of the notice under subsection (4).

(6) If before the expiration of the period mentioned in paragraph (*c*) of subsection (5) the Council offer to enter into an agreement for the acquisition of the interest of the person who gave the notice under subsection (4) or an agreement under section 16 of the 1949 Act or section 15 of the 1968 Act providing for the making by them of payments to that person, that paragraph shall have effect as if for the said period there were substituted—

(*a*) where the agreement is entered into before the expiration of twelve months from the giving of the notice, the period expiring on the day on which it is entered into ;

(*b*) in any other case, twelve months from the giving of the notice or three months from rejection or withdrawal of the offer to enter into the agreement, whichever period last expires.

(7) If before the expiration of the period mentioned in paragraph (*c*) of subsection (5), or that paragraph as it has effect by virtue of subsection (6), an order is made for the compulsory acquisition by the Council of the interest of the person who gave the notice under subsection (4), that paragraph shall have effect as if for the said period there were substituted the period expiring—

(*a*) in the case of an order which is confirmed, on the day on which the Council enter on the land ;

(*b*) in any other case, on the day on which the order is withdrawn or the Secretary of State decides not to confirm it.

(8) A person who, without reasonable excuse, contravenes subsection (3) shall be liable—

(*a*) on summary conviction, to a fine not exceeding the statutory maximum ;

(*b*) on conviction on indictment, to a fine.

(9) It is a reasonable excuse in any event for a person to carry out an operation if—

(*a*) the operation was authorised by a planning permission granted on an application under Part III of the Town and Country Planning Act 1971 or Part III of the Town and Country Planning (Scotland) Act 1972 ; or

1971 c. 78.
1972 c. 52.

(*b*) the operation was an emergency operation particulars of which (including details of the emergency) were notified to the Council as soon as practicable after the commencement of the operation. PART II

(10) An order made under this section in relation to land in Scotland shall be registered either—

(a) in a case where the land affected by the order is registered in that Register, in the Land Register of Scotland ; or

(b) in any other case, in the appropriate Division of the General Register of Sasines.

(11) A report submitted by the Council to the Secretary of State under paragraph 17 of Schedule 3 to the Nature Conservancy Council Act 1973 for any year shall set out particulars of any areas of land as respects which orders under this section have come into operation during that year. 1973 c. 54.

Compensation where order is made under s. 29.

30.—(1) Subsection (2) applies where an order is made under section 29 and subsection (3) applies where—

(a) notice of a proposal to carry out an operation is duly given to the Nature Conservancy Council under subsection (4) of that section ; and

(b) paragraph (c) of subsection (5) of that section has effect as modified by subsection (6) or (7) of that section.

(2) The Council shall pay compensation to any person having at the time of the making of the order an interest in land comprised in an agricultural unit comprising land to which the order relates who, on a claim made to the Council within the time and in the manner prescribed by regulations under this section, shows that the value of his interest is less than what it would have been if the order had not been made ; and the amount of the compensation shall be equal to the difference between the two values.

(3) The Council shall pay compensation to any person having at the time of the giving of the notice an interest in land to which the notice relates who, on a claim made to the Council within the time and in the manner prescribed by regulations under this section, shows that—

(a) he has reasonably incurred expenditure which has been rendered abortive, or expenditure in carrying out work which has been rendered abortive, by reason of paragraph (c) of subsection (5) of section 29 having effect as modified by subsection (6) or (7) of that section ; or

(b) he has incurred loss or damage which is directly attributable to that paragraph having effect as so modified ;

but nothing in this subsection shall entitle any such person to compensation in respect of any reduction in the value of his interest in the land.

PART II

(4) For the purposes of subsection (2)—

(*a*) an interest in land shall be valued as at the time when the order is made;

(*b*) where a person, by reason of his having more than one interest in land, makes more than one claim under that subsection in respect of the same order, his various interests shall be valued together;

1973 c. 26.
1973 c. 56.

(*c*) section 10 of the Land Compensation Act 1973 (mortgages, trusts for sale and settlements) or section 10 of the Land Compensation (Scotland) Act 1973 (restricted interests in land) shall apply in relation to compensation under that subsection as it applies in relation to compensation under Part I of that Act.

1961 c. 33.
1963 c. 51.

(5) For the purposes of assessing any compensation payable under subsection (2), the rules set out in section 5 of the Land Compensation Act 1961 or section 12 of the Land Compensation (Scotland) Act 1963 shall, so far as applicable and subject to any necessary modifications, have effect as they have effect for the purpose of assessing compensation for the compulsory acquisition of an interest in land.

(6) No claim shall be made under subsection (2) in respect of any order under section 29 unless the Secretary of State has given notice under paragraph 6(1) or (2) of Schedule 11 of his decision in respect of the order; and, without prejudice to subsection (4)(*a*), that decision will be taken into account in assessing the compensation payable in respect of the order.

(7) Compensation under this section shall carry interest, at the rate for the time being prescribed under section 32 of the Land Compensation Act 1961 or section 40 of the Land Compensation (Scotland) Act 1963, from the date of the claim until payment.

(8) Except in so far as may be provided by regulations under this section, any question of disputed compensation under this section shall be referred to and determined by the Lands Tribunal or the Lands Tribunal for Scotland.

(9) In relation to the determination of any such question, the provisions of sections 2 and 4 of the Land Compensation Act 1961 or sections 9 and 11 of the Land Compensation (Scotland) Act 1963 (procedure and costs) shall apply, subject to any necessary modifications and to the provisions of any regulations under this section.

(10) Regulations under this section shall be made by the Secretary of State and shall be made by statutory instrument subject to annulment in pursuance of a resolution of either House of Parliament.

PART II

(11) In this section " agricultural unit " means land which is occupied as a unit for agricultural purposes, including any dwelling-house or other building occupied by the same person for the purpose of farming the land.

Restoration where order under s. 29 is contravened.

31.—(1) Where the operation in respect of which a person is convicted of an offence under section 29 has destroyed or damaged any of the flora, fauna, or geological or physiographical features by reason of which the land on which it was carried out is of special interest, the court by which he is convicted, in addition to dealing with him in any other way, may make an order requiring him to carry out, within such period as may be specified in the order, such operations for the purpose of restoring the land to its former condition as may be so specified.

(2) An order under this section made on conviction on indictment shall be treated for the purposes of sections 30 and 42(1) and (2) of the Criminal Appeal Act 1968 (effect of appeals on orders for the restitution of property) as an order for the restitution of property; and where by reason of the quashing by the Court of Appeal of a person's conviction any such order does not take effect, and on appeal to the House of Lords the conviction is restored by that House, the House may make any order under this section which could be made on his conviction by the court which convicted him.

1968 c. 19.

(3) In the case of an order under this section made by a magistrates' court the period specified in the order shall not begin to run—

(*a*) in any case until the expiration of the period for the time being prescribed by law for the giving of notice of appeal against a decision of a magistrates' court;

(*b*) where notice of appeal is given within the period so prescribed, until determination of the appeal.

(4) At any time before an order under this section has been complied with or fully complied with, the court by which it was made may, on the application of the person against whom it was made, discharge or vary the order if it appears to the court that a change in circumstances has made compliance or full compliance with the order impracticable or unnecessary.

(5) If, within the period specified in an order under this section, the person against whom it was made fails, without reasonable excuse, to comply with it, he shall be liable on summary conviction—

(*a*) to a fine not exceeding £1,000 ; and

(*b*) in the case of a continuing offence, to a further fine not exceeding £100 for each day during which the offence continues after conviction.

PART II

(6) If, within the period specified in an order under this section, any operations specified in the order have not been carried out, the Nature Conservancy Council may enter the land and carry out those operations and recover from the person against whom the order was made any expenses reasonably incurred by them in doing so.

(7) In the application of this section to Scotland—

(*a*) subsections (2) and (3) shall not apply ; and

(*b*) for the purposes of any appeal or review, an order under this section is a sentence.

Duties of agriculture Ministers with respect to areas of special scientific interest.
1970 c. 40.

32.—(1) Where an application for a grant under a scheme made under section 29 of the Agriculture Act 1970 (farm capital grants) is made as respects expenditure incurred or to be incurred for the purpose of activities on land notified under section 28(1) or land to which section 29(3) applies, the appropriate Minister—

(*a*) shall, so far as may be consistent with the purposes of the scheme and section 29 of the said Act of 1970, so exercise his functions thereunder as to further the conservation of the flora, fauna, or geological or physiographical features by reason of which the land is of special interest ; and

(*b*) where the Nature Conservancy Council have objected to the making of the grant on the ground that the activities in question have destroyed or damaged or will destroy or damage that flora or fauna or those features, shall not make the grant except after considering the objection and, in the case of land in England, after consulting with the Secretary of State.

(2) Where, in consequence of an objection by the Council, an application for a grant as respects expenditure to be incurred is refused on the ground that the activities in question will have such an effect as is mentioned in subsection (1)(*b*), the Council shall, within three months of their receiving notice of the appropriate Minister's decision, offer to enter into, in the terms of a draft submitted to the applicant, an agreement under section 16 of the 1949 Act or section 15 of the 1968 Act—

(*a*) imposing restrictions as respects those activities ; and

(*b*) providing for the making by them of payments to the applicant.

(3) In this section " the appropriate Minister " has the same meaning as in section 29 of the said Act of 1970.

PART II

Ministerial guidance as respects areas of special scientific interest.

33.—(1) The Ministers shall from time to time, after consultation with the Nature Conservancy Council and such persons appearing to them to represent other interests concerned as they consider appropriate—

(*a*) prepare codes containing such recommendations, advice and information as they consider proper for the guidance of—

(i) persons exercising functions under sections 28 to 32 ; and

(ii) persons affected or likely to be affected by the exercise of any of those functions ; and

(*b*) revise any such code by revoking, varying, amending or adding to the provisions of the code in such manner as the Ministers think fit.

(2) A code prepared in pursuance of subsection (1) and any alterations proposed to be made on a revision of such a code shall be laid before both Houses of Parliament forthwith after being prepared ; and the code or revised code, as the case may be, shall not be issued until the code or the proposed alterations have been approved by both Houses.

(3) Subject to subsection (2), the Ministers shall cause every code prepared or revised in pursuance of subsection (1) to be printed, and may cause copies of it to be put on sale to the public at such price as the Ministers may determine.

Limestone pavement orders.

34.—(1) Where the Nature Conservancy Council or the Commission are of the opinion that any land in the countryside which comprises a limestone pavement is of special interest by reason of its flora, fauna or geological or physiographical features, it shall be the duty of the Council or the Commission to notify that fact to the local planning authority in whose area the land is situated.

(2) Where it appears to the Secretary of State or the relevant authority that the character or appearance of any land notified under subsection (1) would be likely to be adversely affected by the removal of the limestone or by its disturbance in any way whatever, the Secretary of State or that authority may make an order (in this section referred to as a " limestone pavement order ") designating the land and prohibiting the removal or disturbance of limestone on or in it ; and the provisions of Schedule 11 shall have effect as to the making, confirmation and coming into operation of limestone pavement orders.

(3) The relevant authority may, after consultation with the Council and the Commission, amend or revoke a limestone pavement order made by the authority ; and the Secretary of State may, after such consultation as aforesaid, amend or revoke

PART II

any such order made by him or that authority but, in the case of an order made by that authority, only after consultation with that authority.

(4) If any person without reasonable excuse removes or disturbs limestone on or in any land designated by a limestone pavement order he shall be liable—

(*a*) on summary conviction, to a fine not exceeding the statutory maximum;

(*b*) on conviction on indictment, to a fine.

(5) It is a reasonable excuse in any event for a person to remove or disturb limestone or cause or permit its removal or disturbance, if the removal or disturbance was authorised by a planning permission granted on an application under Part III of the Town and Country Planning Act 1971 or Part III of the Town and Country Planning (Scotland) Act 1972.

1971 c. 78.
1972 c. 52.

(6) In this section—

"the Commission" means the Countryside Commission in relation to England and Wales and the Countryside Commission for Scotland in relation to Scotland;

"limestone pavement" means an area of limestone which lies wholly or partly exposed on the surface of the ground and has been fissured by natural erosion;

"the relevant authority" means the county planning authority in relation to England and Wales and the authority exercising district planning functions in relation to Scotland.

National nature reserves.

35.—(1) Where the Nature Conservancy Council are satisfied that any land which—

(*a*) is being managed as a nature reserve under an agreement entered into with the Council;

(*b*) is held by the Council and is being managed by them as a nature reserve; or

(*c*) is held by an approved body and is being managed by that body as a nature reserve,

is of national importance, they may declare that land to be a national nature reserve.

(2) A declaration by the Council that any land is a national nature reserve shall be conclusive of the matters declared; and subsections (4) and (5) of section 19 of the 1949 Act shall apply in relation to any such declaration as they apply in relation to a declaration under that section.

(3) On the application of the approved body concerned, the Council may, as respects any land which is declared to be a national nature reserve under subsection (1)(*c*), make byelaws for the protection of the reserve.

(4) Subsections (2) and (3) of section 20 and section 106 of the 1949 Act shall apply in relation to byelaws under this section as they apply in relation to byelaws under the said section 20. PART II

(5) In this section—

" approved body " means a body approved by the Council for the purposes of this section;

" nature reserve " has the same meaning as in Part III of the 1949 Act.

Marine nature reserves.

36.—(1) Where, in the case of any land covered (continuously or intermittently) by tidal waters or parts of the sea in or adjacent to Great Britain up to the seaward limits of territorial waters, it appears to the Secretary of State expedient, on an application made by the Nature Conservancy Council, that the land and waters covering it should be managed by the Council for the purpose of—

(*a*) conserving marine flora or fauna or geological or physiographical features of special interest in the area; or

(*b*) providing, under suitable conditions and control, special opportunities for the study of, and research into, matters relating to marine flora and fauna and the physical conditions in which they live, or for the study of geological and physiographical features of special interest in the area,

he may by order designate the area comprising that land and those waters as a marine nature reserve; and the Council shall manage any area so designated for either or both of those purposes.

(2) An application for an order under this section shall be accompanied by—

(*a*) a copy of the byelaws which, if an order is made, the Council propose making under section 37 for the protection of the area specified in the application; and

(*b*) a copy of any byelaws made or proposed to be made for the protection of that area by a relevant authority;

and an order made on the application shall authorise the making under that section of such of the byelaws proposed to be made by the Council as may be set out in the order with or without modifications.

(3) Byelaws the making of which is so authorised—

(*a*) shall not require the Secretary of State's consent under subsection (1) of section 37; and

(*b*) notwithstanding anything in the provisions applied by subsection (4) of that section, shall take effect on their being made.

PART II

(4) The provisions of Schedule 12 shall have effect as to the making, validity and date of coming into operation of orders under this section ; and an order made under this section may be amended or revoked by a subsequent order so made.

(5) The powers exercisable by the Council for the purpose of managing an area designated as a marine nature reserve under this section shall include power to install markers indicating the existence and extent of the reserve.

(6) Nothing in this section or in byelaws made under section 37 shall interfere with the exercise of any functions of a relevant authority, any functions conferred by or under an enactment (whenever passed) or any right of any person (whenever vested).

(7) In this section—

" enactment " includes an enactment contained in a local Act ;

" local authority " means—

(*a*) in relation to England and Wales, a county council, a district council, the Greater London Council or a London borough council ;

(*b*) in relation to Scotland, a regional council, an islands council or a district council ;

" relevant authority " means a local authority, a water authority or any other statutory water undertakers, an internal drainage board, a navigation authority, a harbour authority, a pilotage authority, a lighthouse authority, a conservancy authority, a river purification board, a district board for a fishery district within the meaning of the Salmon Fisheries (Scotland) Act 1862, or a local fisheries committee constituted under the Sea Fisheries Regulation Act 1966.

1862 c. 97.

1966 c. 38.

Byelaws for protection of marine nature reserves.

37.—(1) The Nature Conservancy Council may, with the consent of the Secretary of State make byelaws for the protection of any area designated as a marine nature reserve under section 36.

(2) Without prejudice to the generality of subsection (1), byelaws made under this section as respects a marine nature reserve—

(*a*) may provide for prohibiting or restricting, either absolutely or subject to any exceptions—

(i) the entry into, or movement within, the reserve of persons and vessels ;

(ii) the killing, taking, destruction, molestation or disturbance of animals or plants of any description in the reserve, or the doing of anything therein which will interfere with the sea bed or damage or disturb any object in the reserve ; or **PART II**

(iii) the depositing of rubbish in the reserve ;

(*b*) may provide for the issue, on such terms and subject to such conditions as may be specified in the byelaws, of permits authorising entry into the reserve or the doing of anything which would otherwise be unlawful under the byelaws ; and

(*c*) may be so made as to apply either generally or with respect to particular parts of the reserve or particular times of the year.

(3) Nothing in byelaws made under this section shall—

(*a*) prohibit or restrict the exercise of any right of passage by a vessel other than a pleasure boat ; or

(*b*) prohibit, except with respect to particular parts of the reserve at particular times of the year, the exercise of any such right by a pleasure boat.

(4) Nothing in byelaws so made shall make unlawful—

(*a*) anything done for the purpose of securing the safety of any vessel, or of preventing damage to any vessel or cargo, or of saving life ;

(*b*) the discharge of any substance from a vessel ; or

(*c*) anything done more than 30 metres below the sea bed.

(5) Sections 236 to 238 of the Local Government Act 1972 or sections 202 to 204 of the Local Government (Scotland) Act 1973 (which relate to the procedure for making byelaws, authorise byelaws to impose fines not exceeding the amount there specified and provide for the proof of byelaws in legal proceedings) shall apply to byelaws under this section as if the Council were a local authority within the meaning of the said Act of 1972 or the said Act of 1973, so however that in relation to such byelaws the said sections shall apply subject to such modifications (including modifications increasing the maximum fines which the byelaws may impose) as may be prescribed by regulations made by the Secretary of State. 1972 c. 70. 1973 c. 65.

Regulations under this subsection shall be made by statutory instrument which shall be subject to annulment in pursuance of a resolution of either House of Parliament.

(6) In relation to byelaws under this section the confirming authority for the purposes of the said section 236 or the said section 202 shall be the Secretary of State.

PART II

(7) The Secretary of State may, after consultation with the Council, direct them—

(*a*) to revoke any byelaws previously made under this section ; or

(*b*) to make any such amendments of any byelaws so made as may be specified in the direction.

(8) The Council shall have power to enforce byelaws made under this section ; but nothing in this subsection shall be construed as authorising the Council to institute proceedings in Scotland for an offence.

(9) Proceedings in England and Wales for an offence under byelaws made under this section shall not, without the consent of the Director of Public Prosecutions, be taken by a person other than the Council.

(10) In this section " vessel " includes a hovercraft and any aircraft capable of landing on water and " pleasure boat " shall be construed accordingly.

(11) References in this section to animals or plants of any description include references to eggs, seeds, spores, larvae or other immature stages of animals or plants of that description.

Grants and loans by Nature Conservancy Council.

38.—(1) The Nature Conservancy Council may, with the consent of, or in accordance with a general authorisation given by, the Secretary of State, give financial assistance by way of grant or loan, or partly in the one way and partly in the other, to any person in respect of expenditure incurred or to be incurred by him in doing anything which, in their opinion, is conducive to nature conservation or fostering the understanding of nature conservation.

(2) No consent or general authorisation shall be given by the Secretary of State under subsection (1) without the approval of the Treasury.

(3) On making a grant or loan under this section the Council may impose such conditions as they think fit including (in the case of a grant) conditions for repayment in specified circumstances.

(4) The Council shall so exercise their powers under subsection (3) as to ensure that any person receiving a grant or loan under this section in respect of premises to which the public are to be admitted, whether on payment or otherwise, shall, in the means of access both to and within the premises, and in the parking facilities and sanitary conveniences to be

available (if any), make provision, so far as it is in the circumstances both practicable and reasonable, for the needs of members of the public visiting the premises who are disabled. **PART II**

(5) The exercise of the Council's powers under this section shall be subject to any direction given to the Council by the Secretary of State.

(6) Section 3 of the Nature Conservancy Council Act 1973 (which is superseded by this section) shall cease to have effect. **1973 c. 54.**

Countryside

Management agreements with owners and occupiers of land.

39.—(1) A relevant authority may, for the purpose of conserving or enhancing the natural beauty or amenity of any land which is both in the countryside and within their area or promoting its enjoyment by the public, make an agreement (in this section referred to as a " management agreement ") with any person having an interest in the land with respect to the management of the land during a specified term or without limitation of the duration of the agreement.

(2) Without prejudice to the generality of subsection (1), a management agreement—

(*a*) may impose on the person having an interest in the land restrictions as respects the method of cultivating the land, its use for agricultural purposes or the exercise of rights over the land and may impose obligations on that person to carry out works or agricultural or forestry operations or do other things on the land ;

(*b*) may confer on the relevant authority power to carry out works for the purpose of performing their functions under the 1949 Act and the 1968 Act ; and

(*c*) may contain such incidental and consequential provisions (including provisions for the making of payments by either party to the other) as appear to the relevant authority to be necessary or expedient for the purposes of the agreement.

(3) The provisions of a management agreement with any person interested in the land shall, unless the agreement otherwise provides, be binding on persons deriving title under or from that person and be enforceable by the relevant authority against those persons accordingly.

(4) Schedule 2 to the Forestry Act 1967 (power for tenant for life and others to enter into forestry dedication covenants) shall apply to management agreements as it applies to forestry dedication covenants. **1967 c. 10.**

PART II

(5) In this section " the relevant authority " means—

(*a*) as respects land in a National Park, the county planning authority ;

(*b*) as respects land in Greater London, the Greater London Council or the London borough council ; and

(*c*) as respects any other land, the local planning authority.

(6) The powers conferred by this section on a relevant authority shall be in addition to and not in derogation of any powers conferred on such an authority by or under any enactment.

Experimental schemes.

40. For subsections (1) and (2) of section 4 of the 1968 Act (under which the Countryside Commission may submit for the Secretary of State's approval proposals for experimental schemes in relation to particular areas and are required to carry out proposals approved by him) there shall be substituted the following subsection—

" (1) The Commission, after consultation with such local authorities and other bodies as appear to the Commission to have an interest, may from time to time make and carry out or promote the carrying out of any experimental scheme designed to facilitate the enjoyment of the countryside, or to conserve or enhance its natural beauty or amenity, which—

(*a*) in relation to the countryside generally or to any particular area involves the development or application of new methods, concepts or techniques, or the application or further development of existing methods, concepts or techniques ; and

(*b*) is designed to illustrate the appropriateness of the scheme in question for the countryside generally or for any particular area."

Duties of agriculture Ministers with respect to the countryside.

1944 c. 28.

41.—(1) The advice for the giving of which free of charge the Minister of Agriculture, Fisheries and Food and the Secretary of State are required by section 1(1) of the Agriculture (Miscellaneous Provisions) Act 1944 to make provision through such organisation as they consider appropriate shall include—

(*a*) advice to persons carrying on agricultural businesses on the conservation and enhancement of the natural beauty and amenity of the countryside ;

(*b*) advice to such persons on diversification into other enterprises of benefit to the rural economy ; and

(*c*) advice to government departments and other bodies exercising statutory functions on the promotion and furtherance of such diversification as is mentioned in paragraph (*b*).

(2) In the exercise of his general duty under section 4(2) of the Small Landholders (Scotland) Act 1911 of promoting the interests of agriculture and other rural industries, and without prejudice to the generality of that duty, the Secretary of State shall make provision, through such organisation as he considers appropriate, for the giving of such advice as is mentioned in paragraphs (*a*), (*b*) and (*c*) of subsection (1). PART II 1911 c. 49.

(3) Where an application for a grant under a scheme made under section 29 of the Agriculture Act 1970 (farm capital grants) is made as respects expenditure incurred or to be incurred for the purposes of activities on land which is in a National Park or an area specified for the purposes of this subsection by the Ministers, the appropriate Minister— 1970 c. 40

(*a*) shall, so far as may be consistent with the purposes of the scheme and the said section 29, so exercise his functions thereunder as to further the conservation and enhancement of the natural beauty and amenity of the countryside and to promote its enjoyment by the public ; and

(*b*) where the relevant authority have objected to the making of the grant on the ground that the activities in question have had or will have an adverse effect on the natural beauty or amenity of the countryside or its enjoyment by the public, shall not make the grant except after considering the objection and, in the case of land in England, after consulting with the Secretary of State ;

and this subsection shall have effect, in its application to Scotland, as if references to the amenity of the countryside were omitted.

(4) Where, in consequence of an objection by the relevant authority, an application for a grant as respects expenditure to be incurred is refused on the ground that the activities in question will have such an effect as is mentioned in subsection (3)(*b*), the relevant authority shall, within three months of their receiving notice of the appropriate Minister's decision, offer to enter into, in the terms of a draft submitted to the applicant, a management agreement—

(*a*) imposing restrictions as respects those activities ; and

(*b*) providing for the making by them of payments to the applicant.

(5) In this section—

" agricultural business " and " the appropriate Minister " have the same meanings as in the said section 29 ;

PART II

"management agreement"—

(*a*) in relation to England and Wales, means an agreement under section 39;

1967 c. 86.

(*b*) in relation to Scotland, means an agreement under section 49A of the Countryside (Scotland) Act 1967;

"the relevant authority"—

(*a*) in relation to England and Wales, has the same meaning as in section 39;

(*b*) in relation to Scotland, means the authority exercising district planning functions.

(6) Subsection (1) extends only to England and Wales and subsection (2) extends only to Scotland.

National Parks

Notification of agricultural operations on moor and heath in National Parks.

42.—(1) The Ministers may, if satisfied that it is expedient to do so, by order apply subsection (2) to any land which is comprised in a National Park and which appears to them to consist of or include moor or heath.

(2) Subject to subsection (3), no person shall—

(*a*) by ploughing or otherwise convert into agricultural land any land to which this subsection applies and which is moor or heath which has not been agricultural land at any time within the preceding 20 years; or

(*b*) carry out on any such land any other agricultural operation or any forestry operation which (in either case) appears to the Ministers to be likely to affect its character or appearance and is specified in the order applying this subsection to that land.

(3) Subsection (2) shall not apply in relation to any operation carried out, or caused or permitted to be carried out, by the owner or occupier of the land if—

(*a*) one of them has, after the coming into force of the order, given the county planning authority written notice of a proposal to carry out the operation, specifying its nature and the land on which it is proposed to carry it out; and

(*b*) one of the conditions specified in subsection (4) is satisfied.

(4) The said conditions are—

(*a*) that the county planning authority have given their consent to the carrying out of the operation;

(*b*) where that authority have neither given nor refused their consent, that three months have expired from the giving of the notice; and

PART II

(*c*) where that authority have refused their consent, that twelve months have expired from the giving of the notice.

(5) A person who, without reasonable excuse, contravenes subsection (2) shall be liable—

(*a*) on summary conviction, to a fine not exceeding the statutory maximum ;

(*b*) on conviction on indictment, to a fine.

(6) Where the county planning authority are given notice under this section in respect of any land, the authority shall forthwith send copies of the notice to the Ministers, the Nature Conservancy Council and the Countryside Commission.

(7) In considering for the purposes of this section whether land has been agricultural land within the preceding 20 years, no account shall be taken of any conversion of the land into agricultural land which was unlawful under the provisions of this section or section 14 of the 1968 Act.

(8) An order under this section shall be made by statutory instrument which shall be subject to annulment in pursuance of a resolution of either House of Parliament.

(9) The said section 14 (which is superseded by this section) shall cease to have effect ; but this section shall have effect as if any order under that section in force immediately before the coming into force of this section had been made under this section.

Maps of National Parks showing certain areas of moor or heath.

43.—(1) Every county planning authority whose area comprises the whole or any part of a National Park shall—

(*a*) before the expiration of the period of two years beginning with the commencement date, prepare a map of the Park or the part thereof showing any areas of moor or heath the natural beauty of which it is, in the opinion of the authority, particularly important to conserve ; and

(*b*) at such intervals thereafter as they think fit (but not less than once in any year), review the particulars contained in the map and make such revisions thereof (if any) as may be requisite.

(2) The authority shall cause a map prepared or revised in pursuance of subsection (1) to be printed, and shall cause copies thereof to be put on sale to the public at such price as the authority may determine.

PART II

Grants and loans for purposes of National Parks.

44.—(1) Without prejudice to section 11 of the 1949 Act (general powers of local planning authorities in relation to National Parks), a county planning authority may give financial assistance by way of grant or loan, or partly in one way and partly in the other, to any person in respect of expenditure incurred by him in doing anything which in the opinion of the authority is conducive to the attainment, in any National Park the whole or part of which is comprised in that authority's area, of any of the following purposes, that is to say, the conservation and enhancement of the natural beauty of that Park and the promotion of its enjoyment by the public.

(2) On making a grant or loan under this section a county planning authority may impose such conditions as they think fit, including (in the case of a grant) conditions for repayment in specified circumstances.

(3) A county planning authority shall so exercise their powers under subsection (2) as to ensure that any person receiving a grant or loan under this section in respect of premises to which the public are to be admitted, whether on payment or otherwise, shall, in the means of access both to and within the premises, and in the parking facilities and sanitary conveniences to be available (if any), make provision, insofar as it is in the circumstances both practicable and reasonable, for the needs of members of the public visiting the premises who are disabled.

Power to vary order designating National Park.

45. The Countryside Commission (as well as the Secretary of State) shall have power to make an order amending an order made under section 5 of the 1949 Act designating a National Park, and—

(*a*) section 7(5) and (6) of that Act (consultation and publicity in connection with orders under section 5 or 7) shall apply to an order under this section as they apply to an order under section 7(4) of that Act with the substitution for the reference in section 7(5) to the Secretary of State of a reference to the Countryside Commission ; and

(*b*) Schedule 1 to that Act (procedure in connection with the making and confirmation of orders under section 5 or 7) shall apply to an order under this section as it applies to an order designating a National Park.

Membership of National Park authorities

1972 c. 70.

46.—(1) In Part I of Schedule 17 to the Local Government Act 1972 (discharge of planning and countryside functions in National Parks) in paragraph 11 after the words " one third " there shall be inserted the words " (to the nearest whole number) ".

PART II

(2) After paragraph 12 of that Schedule there shall be inserted the following paragraph—

" 12A.—(1) The members of a joint planning board, special planning board or National Park Committee established for an area being or comprising the whole or any part of a National Park shall include members (in this paragraph referred to as ' district council members ') who are appointed by district councils whose districts comprise any part of that Park (in this paragraph referred to as ' relevant district councils ').

(2) The number of district council members of such a board or Committee shall be equal to—

(*a*) the number of relevant district councils ; or

(*b*) one seventh (to the nearest whole number) of the members of the board or Committee,

whichever is the less ; and for the purposes of this sub-paragraph any casual vacancy in the membership of the board or Committee shall be disregarded.

(3) The district council members shall be appointed by such of the relevant district councils as may be agreed between those councils or as in default of agreement may be determined by the Secretary of State.

(4) The district council members shall hold office for a period of one year and shall be eligible for reappointment ; and section 102 (5) above shall apply in relation to a district council member appointed under this paragraph as it applies in relation to a member of a committee appointed under that section."

(3) In paragraph 14 of that Schedule for the words " subject to paragraph 11 above " there shall be substituted the words " subject to paragraphs 11 and 12A above ".

(4) In the case of a joint planning board, special planning board or National Park Committee established for an area being or comprising the whole or any part of a National Park, members who are members of relevant district councils (within the meaning of the said paragraph 12A) and are neither members of a county council nor persons appointed in pursuance of the said paragraph 11 shall cease to be members of the board or Committee as from the coming into force of this section.

Miscellaneous and supplemental

Provisions with respect to the Countryside Commission.

47.—(1) Schedule 13 shall have effect as respects the Countryside Commission.

(2) The Secretary of State may, with the approval of the Treasury, make to the Countryside Commission out of moneys

PART II

provided by Parliament grants of such amount and subject to such conditions (if any) as he may, with the approval of the Treasury, think fit.

(3) Sections 2, 4 and 95 of the 1949 Act and section 3 of the 1968 Act (which are superseded by this section) shall cease to have effect.

Duties of water authorities etc. with regard to nature conservation and the countryside.

1973 c. 37.

48.—(1) For subsection (1) of section 22 of the Water Act 1973 (duties with respect to nature conservation and amenity) there shall be substituted the following subsection—

"(1) In formulating or considering any proposals relating to the discharge of any of the functions of water authorities, those authorities and the appropriate Minister or Ministers—

(*a*) shall, so far as may be consistent with the purposes of this Act and of the Land Drainage Act 1976, so exercise their functions with respect to the proposals as to further the conservation and enhancement of natural beauty and the conservation of flora, fauna and geological or physiographical features of special interest;

(*b*) shall have regard to the desirability of protecting buildings or other objects or archaeological, architectural or historic interest; and

(*c*) shall take into account any effect which the proposals would have on the beauty of, or amenity in, any rural or urban area or on any such flora, fauna, features, buildings or objects."

(2) In subsection (3) of that section the words "not being land for the time being managed as a nature reserve" shall be omitted.

(3) After that subsection there shall be inserted the following subsections—

"(4) Where any land has been notified to a water authority under subsection (3) above, the authority shall consult with the Council before executing or carrying out any works or operations appearing to them to be likely to destroy or damage any of the flora, fauna, or geological or physiographical features by reason of which the land is of special interest.

(5) Subsection (4) above shall not apply in relation to any emergency operation particulars of which (including details of the emergency) are notified to the Council as soon as practicable after the commencement of the operation.

(6) References in this section to water authorities shall include references to internal drainage boards and the reference in subsection (3) above to the water authority in whose area the land is situated shall include a reference to the internal drainage board in whose district the land is situated."

Extension of power to appoint wardens.

49.—(1) This section applies to any land in a National Park or in the countryside if—

(*a*) the public are allowed access to the land ; and

(*b*) there is no power under any of the provisions of the 1949 Act and the 1968 Act for a local authority, a local planning authority or the Countryside Commission to appoint wardens as respects that land.

(2) Subject to subsections (3) and (4) the power conferred on a local authority by section 92(1) of the 1949 Act (appointment of wardens) shall include a power, exercisable only with the agreement of the owner and of the occupier of any land to which this section applies, to appoint persons to act as wardens as respects that land.

(3) The only purpose for which wardens may be appointed by virtue of subsection (2) is to advise and assist the public.

(4) Notwithstanding the provisions of section 41(8) of the 1968 Act (Countryside Commission to be local authority for purposes of section 92 of the 1949 Act), nothing in this section shall be construed as conferring on the Countryside Commission any additional power to appoint wardens.

Payments under certain agreements offered by authorities.

50.—(1) This section applies where—

(*a*) the Nature Conservancy Council offer to enter into an agreement under section 16 of the 1949 Act or section 15 of the 1968 Act providing for the making by them of payments to—

(i) a person who has given notice under section 28(5) or 29(4) ; or

(ii) a person whose application for farm capital grant has been refused in consequence of an objection by the Council ; or

(*b*) the relevant authority offer to enter into a management agreement providing for the making by them of payments to a person whose application for a farm capital grant has been refused in consequence of an objection by the authority.

PART II

(2) Subject to subsection (3), the said payments shall be of such amounts as may be determined by the offeror in accordance with guidance given by the Ministers.

(3) If the offeree so requires within one month of receiving the offer, the determination of those amounts shall be referred to an arbitrator (or, in Scotland, an arbiter) to be appointed, in default of agreement, by the Secretary of State; and where the amounts determined by the arbitrator exceed those determined by the offeror, the offeror shall—

(*a*) amend the offer so as to give effect to the arbitrator's (or, in Scotland, the arbiter's) determination; or

(*b*) except in the case of an offer made to a person whose application for a farm capital grant has been refused in consequence of an objection by the offeror, withdraw the offer.

(4) In this section—

"farm capital grant" means a grant under a scheme made under section 29 of the Agriculture Act 1970; 1970 c. 40.

"management agreement" and "the relevant authority" have the same meanings as in section 41.

Powers of entry.

51.—(1) Any person authorised in writing by the relevant authority may, at any reasonable time and (if required to do so) upon producing evidence that he is authorised, enter any land for any of the following purposes—

(*a*) to ascertain whether an order should be made in relation to that land under section 29 or if an offence under that section is being, or has been, committed on that land;

(*b*) to ascertain the amount of any compensation payable under section 30 in respect of an interest in that land;

(*c*) to ascertain whether an order should be made in relation to that land under section 34 or if an offence under that section is being, or has been, committed on that land;

(*d*) to ascertain whether an order should be made in relation to that land under section 42 or if an offence under that section is being, or has been, committed on that land;

but nothing in this subsection shall authorise any person to enter a dwelling.

(2) In subsection (1) "the relevant authority" means—

(*a*) for the purposes of paragraphs (*a*) and (*b*) of that subsection, the Nature Conservancy Council;

PART II

(*b*) for the purposes of paragraph (*c*) of that subsection, the Secretary of State or the relevant authority within the meaning of section 34;

(*c*) for the purposes of paragraph (*d*) of that subsection, the Ministers or the county planning authority.

(3) A person shall not demand admission as of right to any land which is occupied unless either—

(*a*) 24 hours notice of the intended entry has been given to the occupier; or

(*b*) the purpose of the entry is to ascertain if an offence under section 29, 34 or 42 is being, or has been, committed on that land.

(4) Any person who intentionally obstructs a person acting in the exercise of any power conferred by subsection (1) shall be liable on summary conviction to a fine not exceeding £200.

Interpretation of Part II.

52.—(1) In this Part, unless the context otherwise requires,—

"agricultural land" does not include land which affords rough grazing for livestock but is not otherwise used as agricultural land;

"the Ministers", in the application of this Part to England, means the Secretary of State and the Minister of Agriculture, Fisheries and Food, and, in the application of this Part to Scotland or Wales, means the Secretary of State.

(2) In the application of this Part to England and Wales—

(*a*) references to a local planning authority shall be construed, except as respects Greater London, as references to a county planning authority and a district planning authority and, as respects Greater London, as references to a London borough council; and

(*b*) references to a county planning authority shall be construed, as respects Greater London, as references to a London borough council;

and in the application of this Part to Scotland references to a local planning authority shall be construed as references to a regional planning authority, a general planning authority and a district planning authority.

(3) References in this Part to the conservation of the natural beauty of any land shall be construed as including references to the conservation of its flora, fauna and geological and physiographical features.

(4) Section 114 of the 1949 Act shall apply for the construction of this Part.

PART II

(5) Any power or duty which under this Part (except sections 41 and 42(1)) falls to be exercised or performed by or in relation to the Ministers may, in England, be exercised or performed by or in relation to either of them.

PART III

PUBLIC RIGHTS OF WAY

Ascertainment of public rights of way

Duty to keep definitive map and statement under continuous review.

53.—(1) In this Part " definitive map and statement ", in relation to any area, means, subject to section 57(3),—

(*a*) the latest revised map and statement prepared in definitive form for that area under section 33 of the 1949 Act; or

(*b*) where no such map and statement have been so prepared, the original definitive map and statement prepared for that area under section 32 of that Act; or

(*c*) where no such map and statement have been so prepared, the map and statement prepared for that area under section 55(3).

(2) As regards every definitive map and statement, the surveying authority shall—

(*a*) as soon as reasonably practicable after the commencement date, by order make such modifications to the map and statement as appear to them to be requisite in consequence of the occurrence, before that date, of any of the events specified in subsection (3); and

(*b*) as from that date, keep the map and statement under continuous review and as soon as reasonably practicable after the occurrence, on or after that date, of any of those events, by order make such modifications to the map and statement as appear to them to be requisite in consequence of the occurrence of that event.

(3) The events referred to in subsection (2) are as follows—

(*a*) the coming into operation of any enactment or instrument, or any other event, whereby—

(i) a highway shown or required to be shown in the map and statement has been authorised to be stopped up, diverted, widened or extended;

(ii) a highway shown or required to be shown in the map and statement as a highway of a particular description has ceased to be a highway of that description; or

(iii) a new right of way has been created over land in the area to which the map relates, being a right of way such that the land over which the right subsists is a public path ; PART III

(*b*) the expiration, in relation to any way in the area to which the map relates, of any period such that the enjoyment by the public of the way during that period raises a presumption that the way has been dedicated as a public path ;

(*c*) the discovery by the authority of evidence which (when considered with all other relevant evidence available to them) shows—

(i) that a right of way which is not shown in the map and statement subsists or is reasonably alleged to subsist over land in the area to which the map relates, being a right of way to which this Part applies ;

(ii) that a highway shown in the map and statement as a highway of a particular description ought to be there shown as a highway of a different description ; or

(iii) that there is no public right of way over land shown in the map and statement as a highway of any description, or any other particulars contained in the map and statement require modification.

(4) The modifications which may be made by an order under subsection (2) shall include the addition to the statement of particulars as to—

(*a*) the position and width of any public path or byway open to all traffic which is or is to be shown on the map ; and

(*b*) any limitations or conditions affecting the public right of way thereover.

(5) Any person may apply to the authority for an order under subsection (2) which makes such modifications as appear to the authority to be requisite in consequence of the occurrence of one or more events falling within paragraph (*b*) or (*c*) of subsection (3) ; and the provisions of Schedule 14 shall have effect as to the making and determination of applications under this subsection.

(6) Orders under subsection (2) which make only such modifications as appear to the authority to be requisite in consequence of the occurrence of one or more events falling within paragraph (*a*) of subsection (3) shall take effect on their being made ; and the provisions of Schedule 15 shall have effect as to the making, validity and date of coming into operation of other orders under subsection (2).

PART III

Duty to reclassify roads used as public paths.

54.—(1) As regards every definitive map and statement, the surveying authority shall, as soon as reasonably practicable after the commencement date,—

(*a*) carry out a review of such of the particulars contained in the map and statement as relate to roads used as public paths; and

(*b*) by order make such modifications to the map and statement as appear to the authority to be requisite to give effect to subsections (2) and (3);

and the provisions of Schedule 15 shall have effect as to the making, validity and date of coming into operation of orders under this subsection.

(2) A definitive map and statement shall show every road used as a public path by one of the three following descriptions, namely—

(*a*) a byway open to all traffic;

(*b*) a bridleway;

(*c*) a footpath,

and shall not employ the expression " road used as a public path " to describe any way.

(3) A road used as a public path shall be shown in the definitive map and statement as follows—

(*a*) if a public right of way for vehicular traffic has been shown to exist, as a byway open to all traffic;

(*b*) if paragraph (*a*) does not apply and public bridleway rights have not been shown not to exist, as a bridleway; and

(*c*) if neither paragraph (*a*) nor paragraph (*b*) applies, as a footpath.

(4) Each way which, in pursuance of an order under subsection (1), is shown in the map and statement by any of the three descriptions shall, as from the coming into operation of the order, be a highway maintainable at the public expense; and each way which, in pursuance of paragraph 9 of Part III of Schedule 3 to the 1968 Act, is so shown shall continue to be so maintainable.

(5) In this section " road used as a public path " means a way which is shown in the definitive map and statement as a road used as a public path.

(6) In subsections (2)(*a*) and (5) of section 51 of the 1949 Act (long distance routes) references to roads used as public paths shall include references to any way shown in a definitive map and statement as a byway open to all traffic.

(7) Nothing in this section or section 53 shall limit the operation of traffic orders under the Road Traffic Regulation Act 1967 or oblige a highway authority to provide, on a way shown in a definitive map and statement as a byway open to all traffic, a metalled carriage-way or a carriage-way which is by any other means provided with a surface suitable for the passage of vehicles. PART III 1967 c. 76.

No further surveys or reviews under the 1949 Act.

55.—(1) No survey under sections 27 to 32 of the 1949 Act, or review under section 33 of that Act, shall be begun after the commencement date; and where on that date a surveying authority have not completed such a survey or review begun earlier, the Secretary of State may, after consultation with the authority, direct the authority—

(*a*) to complete the survey or review; or

(*b*) to abandon the survey or review to such extent as may be specified in the direction.

(2) Where such a survey or review so begun is abandoned, the Secretary of State shall give such notice of the abandonment as appears to him requisite.

(3) Where, in relation to any area, no such survey has been so begun or such a survey so begun is abandoned, the surveying authority shall prepare for that area a map and statement such that, when they have been modified in accordance with the provisions of this Part, they will serve as the definitive map and statement for that area.

(4) Where such a survey so begun is abandoned after a draft map and statement have been prepared and the period for making representations or objections has expired, the authority shall by order modify the map and statement prepared under subsection (3) so as—

(*a*) to give effect to any determination or decision of the authority under section 29(3) or (4) of the 1949 Act in respect of which either there is no right of appeal or no notice of appeal has been duly served ;

(*b*) to give effect to any decision of the Secretary of State under section 29(6) of that Act ; and

(*c*) to show any particulars shown in the draft map and statement with respect to which no representation or objection has been duly made, or in relation to which all such representations or objections had been withdrawn.

(5) Where such a review so begun is abandoned after a draft map and statement have been prepared and the period for making representations or objections has expired, the authority

PART III

shall by order modify the map and statement under review so as—

(*a*) to give effect to any decision of the Secretary of State under paragraph 4(4) of Part II of Schedule 3 to the 1968 Act; and

(*b*) to show any particulars shown in the draft map and statement but not in the map and statement under review, and to omit any particulars shown in the map and statement under review but not in the draft map and statement, being (in either case) particulars with respect to which no representation or objection has been duly made, or in relation to which all such representations or objections have been withdrawn.

(6) Orders under subsection (4) or (5) shall take effect on their being made.

Effect of definitive map and statement.

56.—(1) A definitive map and statement shall be conclusive evidence as to the particulars contained therein to the following extent, namely—

(*a*) where the map shows a footpath, the map shall be conclusive evidence that there was at the relevant date a highway as shown on the map, and that the public had thereover a right of way on foot, so however that this paragraph shall be without prejudice to any question whether the public had at that date any right of way other than that right;

(*b*) where the map shows a bridleway, the map shall be conclusive evidence that there was at the relevant date a highway as shown on the map, and that the public had thereover at that date a right of way on foot and a right of way on horseback or leading a horse, so however that this paragraph shall be without prejudice to any question whether the public had at that date any right of way other than those rights;

(*c*) where the map shows a byway open to all traffic, the map shall be conclusive evidence that there was at the relevant date a highway as shown on the map, and that the public had thereover at that date a right of way for vehicular and all other kinds of traffic;

(*d*) where the map shows a road used as a public path, the map shall be conclusive evidence that there was at the relevant date a highway as shown on the map, and that the public had thereover at that date a right of way on foot and a right of way on horseback or leading a horse, so however that this paragraph shall be without prejudice to any question whether the public had at that date any right of way other than those rights; and PART III

(*e*) where by virtue of the foregoing paragraphs the map is conclusive evidence, as at any date, as to a highway shown thereon, any particulars contained in the statement as to the position or width thereof shall be conclusive evidence as to the position or width thereof at that date, and any particulars so contained as to limitations or conditions affecting the public right of way shall be conclusive evidence that at the said date the said right was subject to those limitations or conditions, but without prejudice to any question whether the right was subject to any other limitations or conditions at that date.

(2) For the purposes of this section " the relevant date "—

(*a*) in relation to any way which is shown on the map otherwise than in pursuance of an order under the foregoing provisions of this Part, means the date specified in the statement as the relevant date for the purposes of the map;

(*b*) in relation to any way which is shown on the map in pursuance of such an order, means the date which, in accordance with subsection (3), is specified in the order as the relevant date for the purposes of the order.

(3) Every order under the foregoing provisions of this Part shall specify, as the relevant date for the purposes of the order, such date, not being earlier than six months before the making of the order, as the authority may determine.

(4) A document purporting to be certified on behalf of the surveying authority to be a copy of or of any part of a definitive map or statement as modified in accordance with the provisions of this Part shall be receivable in evidence and shall be deemed, unless the contrary is shown, to be such a copy.

(5) Where it appears to the Secretary of State that paragraph (*d*) of subsection (1) can have no further application, he may by order made by statutory instrument repeal that paragraph.

Supplementary provisions as to definitive maps and statements.

57.—(1) An order under the foregoing provisions of this Part shall be in such form as may be prescribed by regulations made by the Secretary of State, and shall contain a map, on such scale as may be so prescribed, showing the modifications to which the order relates.

(2) Regulations made by the Secretary of State may prescribe the scale on which maps are to be prepared under section 55(3),

PART III

and the method of showing in definitive maps and statements anything which is required to be so shown.

(3) Where, in the case of a definitive map and statement for any area which have been modified in accordance with the foregoing provisions of this Part, it appears to the surveying authority expedient to do so, they may prepare a copy of that map and statement as so modified; and where they do so, the map and statement so prepared, and not the map and statement so modified, shall be regarded for the purposes of the foregoing provisions of this Part as the definitive map and statement for that area.

(4) The statement prepared under subsection (3) shall specify, as the relevant date for the purposes of the map, such date, not being earlier than six months before the preparation of the map and statement, as the authority may determine.

(5) As regards every definitive map and statement, the surveying authority shall keep—

(*a*) a copy of the map and statement; and

(*b*) copies of all orders under this Part modifying the map and statement,

available for inspection free of charge at all reasonable hours at one or more places in each district comprised in the area to which the map and statement relate and, so far as appears practicable to the surveying authority, a place in each parish so comprised; and the authority shall be deemed to comply with the requirement to keep such copies available for inspection in a district or parish if they keep available for inspection there a copy of so much of the map and statement and copies of so many of the orders as relate to the district or parish.

(6) Notwithstanding anything in subsection (5), an authority shall not be required to keep available for inspection more than one copy of—

(*a*) any definitive map and statement; or

(*b*) each order under this Part modifying the map and statement,

if, as respects the area to which that map and statement relate, a subsequent map and statement have been prepared under subsection (3); and the said single copies may be kept in such place in the area of the authority as they may determine.

(7) Every surveying authority shall take such steps as they consider expedient for bringing to the attention of the public the provisions of this Part including, in particular, section 53(5) and subsection (5).

(8) Regulations under this section shall be made by statutory instrument which shall be subject to annulment in pursuance of a resolution of either House of Parliament.

Application of ss. 53 to 57 to inner London.

58.—(1) Subject to subsection (2), the foregoing provisions of this Part shall not apply to any area to which this subsection applies; and this subsection applies to any area which, immediately before 1st April 1965, formed part of the administrative county of London.

(2) A London borough council may by resolution adopt the said foregoing provisions as respects any part of their area specified in the resolution, being a part to which subsection (1) applies, and those provisions shall thereupon apply accordingly.

(3) Where by virtue of a resolution under subsection (2), the said foregoing provisions apply to any area, those provisions shall have effect in relation thereto as if for references to the commencement date there were substituted references to the date on which the resolution comes into operation.

Miscellaneous and supplemental

Prohibition on keeping bulls on land crossed by public rights of way.

59.—(1) If, in a case not falling within subsection (2), the occupier of a field or enclosure crossed by a right of way to which this Part applies permits a bull to be at large in the field or enclosure, he shall be liable on summary conviction to a fine not exceeding £200.

(2) Subsection (1) shall not apply to any bull which—

(*a*) does not exceed the age of ten months; or

(*b*) is not of a recognised dairy breed and is at large in any field or enclosure in which cows or heifers are also at large.

(3) Nothing in any byelaws, whenever made, shall make unlawful any act which is, or but for subsection (2) would be, made unlawful by subsection (1).

(4) In this section " recognised dairy breed " means one of the following breeds, namely, Ayrshire, British Friesian, British Holstein, Dairy Shorthorn, Guernsey, Jersey and Kerry.

(5) The Secretary of State may by order add any breed to, or remove any breed from, subsection (4); and an order under this subsection shall be made by statutory instrument which shall be subject to annulment in pursuance of a resolution of either House of Parliament.

PART III

Regulation of traffic on public rights of way.

1967 c. 76.

60. The Road Traffic Regulation Act 1967 shall have effect in relation to any footpath, bridleway or byway open to all traffic as if—

(*a*) any reference to traffic included a reference to foot passengers and persons driving, riding or leading horses or other animals of draught or burden ; and

(*b*) any reference in section 1(3A) or 12 to foot passengers included a reference to such persons as aforesaid.

Ploughing of public rights of way.

1980 c. 66.

61.—(1) Section 134 of the Highways Act 1980 (ploughing of footpath or bridleway) shall have effect subject to the amendments provided for by subsections (2) to (9).

(2) Subsection (3) (7 days' notice of intention to plough) shall be omitted.

(3) In subsection (4) (duty to restore surface of footpath or bridleway), for paragraphs (*a*) and (*b*) there shall be substituted the following paragraphs—

" (*a*) not later than 2 weeks from the time when the occupier began to plough the footpath or bridleway, or

(*b*) if prevented from doing so by exceptional weather conditions, as soon as practicable thereafter,".

(4) In subsection (5) (failure to comply with subsection (3) or (4)) the words " (3) or " shall be omitted, for paragraphs (*a*) and (*b*) there shall be substituted the words " to a fine not exceeding £200 " and for the words " subsection (4) ", in the second place where they occur, there shall be substituted the words " that subsection ".

(5) After that subsection there shall be inserted the following subsection—

" (5A) A person who ploughs any footpath, bridleway or other highway otherwise than in the exercise of a right to plough it shall be guilty of an offence and liable to a fine not exceeding £200."

(6) In subsection (6) (enforcement of subsections (3) to (5)) for the words " subsections (3) to (5) above as respects any footpath or bridleway " there shall be substituted the words " subsections (4) to (5A) above as respects any footpath, bridleway or other highway ".

(7) In subsection (7) (proceedings by parish or community councils) after the words " subsection (4) " there shall be inserted the words " or (5A) ".

(8) In subsection (8) (power of competent authority to restore surface of footpath or bridleway) for the words " footpath or bridleway " there shall be substituted the words " footpath, bridleway or other highway ".

Part III

(9) In subsection (10) (competent authorities for the purposes of subsections (8) and (9)) for the words " footpath or bridleway ", in both places where they occur, there shall be substituted the words " footpath, bridleway or other highway ".

(10) In section 135(1) of the said Act of 1980 (temporary diversion of footpath or bridleway ploughed up under section 134) the words " 6 or " and " 6 weeks or " shall be omitted.

Appointment of wardens for public rights of way.

62. A local authority may appoint such number of persons as appears to the authority to be necessary or expedient to act as wardens as respects a footpath, bridleway or byway open to all traffic which is both in the countryside and in the area of the authority, and the purpose for which the wardens may be so appointed is to advise and assist the public in connection with the use of the path or way.

Orders creating, extinguishing or diverting footpaths and bridleways.

63. The enactments mentioned in Schedule 16 (which relate to the making and confirmation of certain orders creating, extinguishing or diverting footpaths and bridleways) shall have effect subject to the amendments provided for in that Schedule.

Publication of dedication of footpaths and bridleways.

64. At the end of section 25 of the Highways Act 1980 (creation of footpath or bridleway by agreement) there shall be inserted the following subsection—

1980 c. 66.

" (6) As soon as may be after the dedication of a footpath or bridleway in accordance with a public path creation agreement, the local authority who are party to the agreement shall give notice of the dedication by publication in at least one local newspaper circulating in the area in which the land to which the agreement relates is situated.".

Signposting of byways open to all traffic.

65.—(1) In section 27 of the 1968 Act (signposting of footpaths and bridleways) for the words " or bridleway ", wherever they occur, there shall be substituted the words " bridleway or byway " ; and for the words " and bridleways " in subsection (6) of that section there shall be substituted the words " bridleways and byways ".

(2) After subsection (7) of that section there shall be inserted the following subsection—

" (8) In this section " byway " means a byway open to all traffic, that is to say, a highway over which the public have a right of way for vehicular and all other kinds of traffic, but which is used by the public mainly for the purposes for which footpaths and bridleways are so used."

PART III

Interpretation of Part III.

66. (1) In this Part—

"bridleway" means a highway over which the public have the following, but no other, rights of way, that is to say, a right of way on foot and a right of way on horseback or leading a horse, with or without a right to drive animals of any description along the highway;

"byway open to all traffic" means a highway over which the public have a right of way for vehicular and all other kinds of traffic, but which is used by the public mainly for the purpose for which footpaths and bridleways are so used;

"definitive map and statement" has the meaning given by section 53(1);

"footpath" means a highway over which the public have a right of way on foot only, other than such a highway at the side of a public road;

"horse" includes a pony, ass and mule, and "horseback" shall be construed accordingly;

"public path" means a highway being either a footpath or a bridleway;

"right of way to which this Part applies" means a right of way such that the land over which the right subsists is a public path or a byway open to all traffic ;

"surveying authority", in relation to any area, means the county or London borough council whose area includes that area.

(2) A highway at the side of a river, canal or other inland navigation shall not be excluded from any definition contained in subsection (1) by reason only that the public have a right to use the highway for purposes of navigation, if the highway would fall within that definition if the public had no such right thereover.

(3) The provisions of section 30(1) of the 1968 Act (riding of pedal cycles on bridleways) shall not affect the definition of bridleway in subsection (1) and any rights exercisable by virtue of those provisions shall be disregarded for the purposes of this Part.

PART IV

MISCELLANEOUS AND GENERAL

Application to Crown.

67.—(1) Subject to the following provisions of this section, Part II, except section 51, and Part III shall apply to Crown land, that is to say, land an interest in which belongs to Her Majesty in the right of the Crown or the Duchy of Lancaster or to the Duchy of Cornwall, and land an interest in which belongs to a Government department or is held in trust for Her Majesty for the purposes of a Government department. PART IV

(2) No order shall be made under section 29, 34, 36 or 42 in relation to Crown land unless the appropriate authority has consented to the making of that order.

(3) An agreement under section 39 as respects any interest in Crown land, other than an interest held by or on behalf of the Crown, shall not have effect unless approved by the appropriate authority.

(4) Section 101(11) of the 1949 Act (Crown land) shall apply for the construction of references in this section to the appropriate authority.

Application to the Isles of Scilly.

68. The Secretary of State may, after consultation with the Council of the Isles of Scilly, by order made by statutory instrument provide for the application of the provisions of Part II or III to the Isles of Scilly as if those Isles were a separate county; and any such order may provide for the application of those provisions to those Isles subject to such modifications as may be specified in the order.

Offences by bodies corporate etc.

69.—(1) Where a body corporate is guilty of an offence under this Act and that offence is proved to have been committed with the consent or connivance of, or to be attributable to any neglect on the part of, any director, manager, secretary or other similar officer of the body corporate or any person who was purporting to act in any such capacity he, as well as the body corporate, shall be guilty of that offence and shall be liable to be proceeded against and punished accordingly.

(2) Where the affairs of a body corporate are managed by its members subsection (1) shall apply in relation to the acts and defaults of a member in connection with his functions of management as if he were a director of the body corporate.

Financial provisions.

70.—(1) There shall be defrayed out of money provided by Parliament—

(*a*) any administrative expenses incurred by any Minister of the Crown under this Act; and

(*b*) any increase attributable to the provisions of this Act in the sums payable out of money so provided under any other enactment.

(2) Any sums received by a Minister of the Crown under this Act shall be paid into the Consolidated Fund.

PART IV

General interpretation.

1949 c. 97.

1968 c. 41.

71. In this Act—

" the 1949 Act " means the National Parks and Access to the Countryside Act 1949 ;

" the 1968 Act " means the Countryside Act 1968 ;

" the commencement date ", in relation to any provision of this Act and any area, means the date of the coming into force of that provision in that area ;

" London borough council " includes the Common Council of the City of London ;

" modifications " includes additions, alterations and omissions, and cognate expressions shall be construed accordingly ;

" statutory maximum ", in relation to a fine on summary conviction, means—

1980 c. 43.

(*a*) in England and Wales, the prescribed sum within the meaning of section 32 of the Magistrates' Courts Act 1980 (at the passing of this Act £1,000) ; and

1975 c. 21.

(*b*) in Scotland, the prescribed sum within the meaning of section 289B of the Criminal Procedure (Scotland) Act 1975 (at the passing of this Act £1,000).

Minor amendments.

1935 c. 47.

72.—(1) Section 4 of the Restriction of Ribbon Development Act 1935 (power to fence roads subject to restrictions) shall have effect, in relation to any area in the countryside of which walls of a particular construction are a feature, as if references to fences included references to walls of that construction ; and in exercising their powers under that section in relation to any such area, a highway authority shall have regard to the desirability of exercising the powers conferred by the foregoing provisions of this subsection.

1946 c. 73.

(2) In section 20(2) of the Hill Farming Act 1946 (penalty for contravening regulations with respect to the burning of heather and grass) as originally enacted for the words from " five pounds " onwards there shall be substituted the words " £200 ".

(3) In section 27 of that Act (penalty for contravening the provisions of that Act relating to muirburn) for the words from " five pounds " onwards there shall be substituted the words " £200 ".

1948 c. 45.

(4) In section 39 of the Agriculture (Scotland) Act 1948 for the words " the First Schedule to the Protection of Birds Act 1954 " there shall be substituted the words " Schedule 1 to the Wildlife and Countryside Act 1981 ".

PART IV

(5) In section 11(1) of the 1949 Act (general powers of local planning authorities in relation to National Parks) after the word " accomplishment " there shall be inserted the words " of any ".

(6) In section 74(4) of the Public Health Act 1961 (power to reduce numbers of pigeons and other birds in built-up areas), for the words " the Protection of Birds Act 1954 " there shall be substituted the words " Part I of the Wildlife and Countryside Act 1981 ". 1961 c. 64.

(7) In section 2(8) of the 1968 Act (publicity and information services) for the words from " encouraging " onwards there shall be substituted the words " informing persons resorting to the countryside of their rights and obligations ".

(8) In section 15(1) of that Act (areas of special scientific interest) the words " which is not for the time being managed as a nature reserve but " shall be omitted.

(9) In section 37 of that Act (protection for interests in the countryside) for the words " and the Act of 1949 " there shall be substituted the words " the Act of 1949 and the Wildlife and Countryside Act 1981 ".

(10) The functions of a county council under this Act as a local planning authority shall be included among the functions of such a council to which Part I of Schedule 17 to the Local Government Act 1972 (planning and countryside functions in National Parks) applies. 1972 c. 70.

(11) In section 31(10) of the Highways Act 1980 (dedication of way as highway presumed after public use for 20 years), for the words from " subsection (4) " to " that section " there shall be substituted the words " section 56(1) of the Wildlife and Countryside Act 1981 (which provides that a definitive map and statement " and the words " or of that subsection " onwards shall be omitted. 1980 c. 66.

(12) Section 80 of that Act (power of highway authority to fence highways) shall have effect in relation to any area in the countryside of which walls of a particular construction are a feature, as if references to fences included references to walls of that construction; and in exercising their powers under that section in relation to any such area, a highway authority shall have regard to the desirability of exercising the powers conferred by the foregoing provisions of this subsection.

(13) In section 136(4) of that Act (time when hedges may not be required to be cut or pruned) immediately before the words " between the last day of September and the first day of April " there shall be inserted the word " except ".

PART IV
1981 c. 37.

(14) In section 4(5) of the Zoo Licensing Act 1981 (grant or refusal of licence) the entries relating to the Protection of Birds Acts 1954 to 1967 and the Conservation of Wild Creatures and Wild Plants Act 1975 shall be omitted and there shall be added at the end the following entry—

" Part I of the Wildlife and Countryside Act 1981 ".

Repeals and savings.

73.—(1) The enactments mentioned in Schedule 17 are hereby repealed to the extent specified in the third column of that Schedule.

(2) Nothing in the repeals made by this section shall affect the operation of sections 27 to 32 of the 1949 Act in relation to any survey begun before the commencement date.

(3) Nothing in the repeals made by this section shall affect the operation of sections 33 and 34 of the 1949 Act and Parts II, III and IV of Schedule 3 to the 1968 Act in relation to any review begun before the commencement date.

1975 c. 48.
1973 c. 57.

(4) Notwithstanding the repeal by this section of the Conservation of Wild Creatures and Wild Plants Act 1975, section 9 of the Badgers Act 1973 shall continue to have effect with the amendment made by section 16 of the said Act of 1975.

Short title commencement and extent.

74.—(1) This Act may be cited as the Wildlife and Countryside Act 1981.

(2) The following provisions of this Act, namely—

Part II, except sections 29 to 32, 41 and 46 to 48 and Schedule 13 ;

sections 59 to 62 and 65 and 66 ; and

Part IV, except section 72(4), (6) and (14) and section 73(1) so far as relating to Part II of Schedule 17,

shall come into force on the expiration of the period of one month beginning with the passing of this Act.

(3) The remaining provisions of this Act shall come into force on such day as the Secretary of State may by order made by statutory instrument appoint and different days may be appointed under this subsection for different provisions, different purposes or different areas.

(4) An order under subsection (3) may make such transitional provision as appears to the Secretary of State to be necessary or expedient in connection with the provisions thereby brought into force.

(5) The following provisions of this Act, namely— PART IV

sections 39, 40 and 42 to 49 and Schedule 13; and Part III,

do not extend to Scotland.

(6) This Act, except section 15(1) and Schedule 10 and, so far as regards any enactment mentioned in Schedule 17 that so extends, section 73 and that Schedule, does not extend to Northern Ireland.

Sections 1, 2, 4, 6, 19 and 22.

SCHEDULES

SCHEDULE 1

Birds which are Protected by Special Penalties

Part I

At All Times

Common name	*Scientific name*
Avocet	Recurvirostra avosetta
Bee-eater	Merops apiaster
Bittern	Botaurus stellaris
Bittern, Little	Ixobrychus minutus
Bluethroat	Luscinia svecica
Brambling	Fringilla montifringilla
Bunting, Cirl	Emberiza cirlus
Bunting, Lapland	Calcarius lapponicus
Bunting, Snow	Plectrophenax nivalis
Buzzard, Honey	Pernis apivorus
Chough	Pyrrhocorax pyrrhocorax
Corncrake	Crex crex
Crake, Spotted	Porzana porzana
Crossbills (all species)	Loxia
Curlew, Stone	Burhinus oedicnemus
Divers (all species)	Gavia
Dotterel	Charadrius morinellus
Duck, Long-tailed	Clangula hyemalis
Eagle, Golden	Aquila chrysaetos
Eagle, White-tailed	Haliaetus albicilla
Falcon, Gyr	Falco rusticolus
Fieldfare	Turdus pilaris
Firecrest	Regulus ignicapillus
Garganey	Anas querquedula
Godwit, Black-tailed	Limosa limosa
Goshawk	Accipiter gentilis
Grebe, Black-necked	Podiceps nigricollis
Grebe, Slavonian	Podiceps auritus
Greenshank	Tringa nebularia
Gull, Little	Larus minutus
Gull, Mediterranean	Larus melanocephalus
Harriers (all species)	Circus
Heron, Purple	Ardea purpurea
Hobby	Falco subbuteo
Hoopoe	Upupa epops
Kingfisher	Alcedo atthis
Kite, Red	Milvus milvus
Merlin	Falco columbarius
Oriole, Golden	Oriolus oriolus
Osprey	Pandion haliaetus
Owl, Barn	Tyto alba
Owl, Snowy	Nyctea scandiaca

SCH. 1

Common name	*Scientific name*
Peregrine	Falco peregrinus
Petrel, Leach's	Oceanodroma leucorhoa
Phalarope, Red-necked	Phalaropus lobatus
Plover, Kentish	Charadrius alexandrinus
Plover, Little Ringed	Charadrius dubius
Quail, Common	Coturnix coturnix
Redstart, Black	Phoenicurus ochruros
Redwing	Turdus iliacus
Rosefinch, Scarlet	Carpodacus erythrinus
Ruff	Philomachus pugnax
Sandpiper, Green	Tringa ochropus
Sandpiper, Purple	Calidris maritima
Sandpiper, Wood	Tringa glareola
Scaup	Aythya marila
Scoter, Common	Melanitta nigra
Scoter, Velvet	Melanitta fusca
Serin	Serinus serinus
Shorelark	Eremophila alpestris
Shrike, Red-backed	Lanius collurio
Spoonbill	Platalea leucorodia
Stilt, Black-winged	Himantopus himantopus
Stint, Temminck's	Calidris temminckii
Swan, Bewick's	Cygnus bewickii
Swan, Whooper	Cygnus cygnus
Tern, Black	Chlidonias niger
Tern, Little	Sterna albifrons
Tern, Roseate	Sterna dougallii
Tit, Bearded	Panurus biarmicus
Tit, Crested	Parus cristatus
Treecreeper, Short-toed	Certhia brachydactyla
Warbler, Cetti's	Cettia cetti
Warbler, Dartford	Sylvia undata
Warbler, Marsh	Acrocephalus palustris
Warbler, Savi's	Locustella luscinioides
Whimbrel	Numenius phaeopus
Woodlark	Lullula arborea
Wryneck	Jynx torquilla

PART II

DURING THE CLOSE SEASON

Common name	*Scientific name*
Goldeneye	Bucephala clangula
Goose, Greylag (in Outer Hebrides, Caithness, Sutherland and Wester Ross only)	Anser anser
Pintail	Anas acuta

NOTE. The common name or names given in the first column of this Schedule are included by way of guidance only ; in the event of any dispute or proceedings, the common name or names shall not be taken into account.

Sections 2, 3, and 22.

SCHEDULE 2

BIRDS WHICH MAY BE KILLED OR TAKEN

PART I

OUTSIDE THE CLOSE SEASON

Common name	*Scientific name*
Capercaillie	Tetrao urogallus
Coot	Fulica atra
Duck, Tufted	Aythya fuligula
Gadwall	Anas strepera
Goldeneye	Bucephala clangula
Goose, Canada	Branta canadensis
Goose, Greylag	Anser anser
Goose, Pink-footed	Anser brachyrhynchus
Goose, White-fronted (in England and Wales only)	Anser albifrons
Mallard	Anas platyrhynchos
Moorhen	Gallinula chloropus
Pintail	Anas acuta
Plover, Golden	Pluvialis apricaria
Pochard	Aythya ferina
Shoveler	Anas clypeata
Snipe, Common	Gallinago gallinago
Teal	Anas crecca
Wigeon	Anas penelope
Woodcock	Scolopax rusticola

PART II

BY AUTHORISED PERSONS AT ALL TIMES

Common name	*Scientific name*
Crow	Corvus corone
Dove, Collared	Streptopelia decaocto
Gull, Great Black-backed	Larus marinus
Gull, Lesser Black-backed	Larus fuscus
Gull, Herring	Larus argentatus
Jackdaw	Corvus monedula
Jay	Garrulus glandarius
Magpie	Pica pica
Pigeon, Feral	Columba livia
Rook	Corvus frugilegus
Sparrow, House	Passer domesticus
Starling	Sturnus vulgaris
Woodpigeon	Columba palumbus

NOTE. The common name or names given in the first column of this Schedule are included by way of guidance only; in the event of any dispute or proceedings, the common name or names shall not be taken into account.

SCHEDULE 3

Sections 6 and 22

BIRDS WHICH MAY BE SOLD

PART I

ALIVE AT ALL TIMES IF RINGED AND BRED IN CAPTIVITY

Common name	*Scientific name*
Blackbird	Turdus merula
Brambling	Fringilla montifringilla
Bullfinch	Pyrrhula pyrrhula
Bunting, Reed	Emberiza schoeniclus
Chaffinch	Fringilla coelebs
Dunnock	Prunella modularis
Goldfinch	Carduelis carduelis
Greenfinch	Carduelis chloris
Jackdaw	Corvus monedula
Jay	Garrulus glandarius
Linnet	Carduelis cannabina
Magpie	Pica pica
Owl, Barn	Tyto alba
Redpoll	Carduelis flammea
Siskin	Carduelis spinus
Starling	Sturnus vulgaris
Thrush, Song	Turdus philomelos
Twite	Carduelis flavirostris
Yellowhammer	Emberiza citrinella

PART II

DEAD AT ALL TIMES

Common name	*Scientific name*
Pigeon, Feral	Columba livia
Woodpigeon	Columba palumbus

PART III

DEAD FROM 1ST SEPTEMBER TO 28TH FEBRUARY

Common name	*Scientific name*
Capercaillie	Tetrao urogallus
Coot	Fulica atra
Duck, Tufted	Aythya fuligula
Mallard	Anas platyrhynchos
Pintail	Anas acuta
Plover, Golden	Pluvialis apricaria
Pochard	Aythya ferina
Shoveler	Anas clypeata
Snipe, Common	Gallinago gallinago
Teal	Anas crecca
Wigeon	Anas penelope
Woodcock	Scolopax rusticola

NOTE. The common name or names given in the first column of this Schedule are included by way of guidance only ; in the event of any dispute or proceedings, the common name or names shall not be taken into account.

Sections 7 and 22.

SCHEDULE 4

BIRDS WHICH MUST BE REGISTERED AND RINGED IF KEPT IN CAPTIVITY

Common name	*Scientific name*
Avocet	Recurvirostra avosetta
Bee-eater	Merops apiaster
Bittern	Botaurus stellaris
Bittern, Little	Ixobrychus minutus
Bluethroat	Luscinia svecica
Bunting, Cirl	Emberiza cirlus
Bunting, Lapland	Calcarius lapponicus
Bunting, Snow	Plectrophenax nivalis
Chough	Pyrrhocorax pyrrhocorax
Corncrake	Crex crex
Crake, Spotted	Porzana porzana
Crossbills (all species)	Loxia
Curlew, Stone	Burhinus oedicnemus
Divers (all species)	Gavia
Dotterel	Charadrius morinellus
Duck, Long-tailed	Clangula hyemalis
Falcons (all species)	Falconidae
Fieldfare	Turdus pilaris
Firecrest	Regulus ignicapillus
Godwit, Black-tailed	Limosa limosa
Grebe, Black-necked	Podiceps nigricollis
Grebe, Slavonian	Podiceps auritus
Greenshank	Tringa nebularia
Hawks, True (except Old world vultures) that is to say, Buzzards, Eagles, Harriers, Hawks and Kites (all species in each case)	Accipitridae (except the genera Aegypius, Gypaetus, Gypohierax, Gyps, Neophron, Sarcogyps and Trigonoceps)
Hoopoe	Upupa epops
Kingfisher	Alcedo atthis
Oriole, Golden	Oriolus oriolus
Osprey	Pandion haliaetus
Petrel, Leach's	Oceanodroma leucorhoa
Phalarope, Red-necked	Phalaropus lobatus
Plover, Kentish	Charadrius alexandrinus
Plover, Little ringed	Charadrius dubius
Quail, Common	Coturnix coturnix
Redstart, Black	Phoenicurus ochruros
Redwing	Turdus iliacus
Rosefinch, Scarlet	Carpodacus erythrinus
Ruff	Philomachus pugnax
Sandpiper, Green	Tringa ochropus
Sandpiper, Purple	Calidris maritima
Sandpiper, Wood	Tringa glareola
Scoter, Common	Melanitta nigra
Scoter, Velvet	Melanitta fusca
Serin	Serinus serinus
Shorelark	Eremophila alpestris
Shrike, Red-backed	Lanius collurio
Spoonbill	Platalea leucorodia
Stilt, Black-winged	Himantopus himantopus

SCH. 4

Common name	*Scientific name*
Stint, Temminck's	Calidris temminckii
Tern, Black	Chlidonias niger
Tern, Little	Sterna albifrons
Tern, Roseate	Sterna dougallii
Tit, Bearded	Panurus biarmicus
Tit, Crested	Parus cristatus
Treecreeper, Short-toed	Certhia brachydactyla
Warbler, Cetti's	Cettia cetti
Warbler, Dartford	Sylvia undata
Warbler, Marsh	Acrocephalus palustris
Warbler, Savi's	Locustella luscinioides
Whimbrel	Numenius phaeopus
Woodlark	Lullula arborea
Wryneck	Jynx torquilla

NOTE. The common name or names given in the first column of this Schedule are included by way of guidance only ; in the event of any dispute or proceedings, the common name or names shall not be taken into account.

SCHEDULE 5

Sections 9, 10, 22 and 24.

ANIMALS WHICH ARE PROTECTED

Common name	*Scientific name*
Adder (in respect of section 9(5) only)	Vipera berus
Bats, Horseshoe (all species)	Rhinolophidae
Bats, Typical (all species)	Vespertilionidae
Beetle, Rainbow Leaf	Chrysolina cerealis
Burbot	Lota lota
Butterfly, Chequered Skipper	Carterocephalus palaemon
Butterfly, Heath Fritillary	Mellicta athalia (otherwise known as Melitaea athalia)
Butterfly, Large Blue	Maculinea arion
Butterfly, Swallowtail	Papilio machaon
Cricket, Field	Gryllus campestris
Cricket, Mole	Gryllotalpa gryllotalpa
Dolphin, Bottle-nosed	Tursiops truncatus (otherwise known as Tursiops tursio)
Dolphin, Common	Delphinus delphis
Dragonfly, Norfolk Aeshna	Aeshna isosceles
Frog, Common (in respect of section 9(5) only)	Rana temporaria
Grasshopper, Wart-biter	Decticus verrucivorus
Lizard, Sand	Lacerta agilis
Lizard, Viviparous (in respect of section 9(5) only)	Lacerta vivipara
Moth, Barberry Carpet	Pareulype berberata
Moth, Black-veined	Siona lineata (otherwise known as Idaea lineata)
Moth, Essex Emerald	Thetidia smaragdaria
Moth, New Forest Burnet	Zygaena viciae
Moth, Reddish Buff	Acosmetia caliginosa

SCH. 5

Common name	*Scientific name*
Newt, Great Crested (otherwise known as Warty newt)	Triturus cristatus
Newt, Palmate (in respect of section 9(5) only)	Triturus helveticus
Newt, Smooth (in respect of section 9(5) only)	Triturus vulgaris
Otter, Common	Lutra lutra
Porpoise, Harbour (otherwise known as Common porpoise)	Phocaena phocaena
Slow-worm (in respect of section 9(5) only)	Anguis fragilis
Snail, Carthusian	Monacha cartusiana
Snail, Glutinous	Myxas glutinosa
Snail, Sandbowl	Catinella arenaria
Snake, Grass (in respect of section 9(5) only)	Natrix helvetica
Snake, Smooth	Coronella austriaca
Spider, Fen Raft	Dolomedes plantarius
Spider, Ladybird	Eresus niger
Squirrel, Red	Sciurus vulgaris
Toad, Common (in respect of section 9(5) only)	Bufo bufo
Toad, Natterjack	Bufo calamita

NOTE. The common name or names given in the first column of this Schedule are included by way of guidance only; in the event of any dispute or proceedings, the common name or names shall not be taken into account.

Sections 11 and 22.

SCHEDULE 6

ANIMALS WHICH MAY NOT BE KILLED OR TAKEN BY CERTAIN METHODS

Common name	*Scientific name*
Badger	Meles meles
Bats, Horseshoe (all species)	Rhinolophidae
Bats, Typical (all species)	Vespertilionidae
Cat, Wild	Felis silvestris
Dolphin, Bottle-nosed	Tursiops truncatus (otherwise known as Tursiops tursio)
Dolphin, Common	Delphinus delphis
Dormice (all species)	Gliridae
Hedgehog	Erinaceus europaeus
Marten, Pine	Martes martes
Otter, Common	Lutra lutra
Polecat	Mustela putorius

SCH. 6

Common name	*Scientific name*
Porpoise, Harbour (otherwise known as Common porpoise)	Phocaena phocaena
Shrews (all species)	Soricidae
Squirrel, Red	Sciurus vulgaris

NOTE. The common name or names given in the first column of this Schedule are included by way of guidance only ; in the event of any dispute or proceedings, the common name or names shall not be taken into account.

SCHEDULE 7

Section 12.

PROTECTION OF CERTAIN MAMMALS

The Ground Game Act 1880

1.—(1) Notwithstanding the provisions of section 6 of the Ground Game Act 1880, it shall not be unlawful for the occupier of any land himself, or one other person authorised by him under section 1 of that Act, to use firearms for the purpose of killing ground game thereon between the expiration of the first hour after sunset and the commencement of the last hour before sunrise if (except where he has the exclusive right) the occupier has the written authority of the other person or one of the other persons entitled to kill and take the ground game on the land. 1880 c. 47.

(2) In this paragraph " ground game " means hares and rabbits.

The Agriculture (Scotland) Act 1948

2.—(1) Notwithstanding the provisions of section 50(1)(*a*) of the Agriculture (Scotland) Act 1948, it shall not be unlawful for the owner of the shooting rights on any land or any person holding those rights from him, or subject to sub-paragraph (2) below the occupier of any land, to use a firearm for the purpose of killing ground game thereon between the expiration of the first hour after sunset and the commencement of the last hour before sunrise. 1948 c. 45.

(2) The occupier of any land shall not use a firearm as mentioned in sub-paragraph (1) above unless (except where he has the exclusive right) he has first obtained the written authority of the other person or one of the other persons entitled to kill and take the ground game on the land.

(3) An occupier who is entitled, in terms of this paragraph, to use a firearm for the purpose of killing ground game may, subject to the provisions of section 1 of the Ground Game Act 1880, authorise one other person so to use a firearm.

(4) In this paragraph " ground game " means hares and rabbits.

SCH. 7

The Dogs (Protection of Livestock) Act 1953

1953 c. 28.

3.—(1) At the end of subsection (2) of section 1 of the Dogs (Protection of Livestock) Act 1953 (penalty where dog worries livestock on agricultural land) there shall be inserted the words " or

(*c*) being at large (that is to say not on a lead or otherwise under close control) in a field or enclosure in which there are sheep ".

(2) After that subsection there shall be inserted the following subsection—

" (2A) Subsection (2)(*c*) of this section shall not apply in relation to—

(*a*) a dog owned by, or in the charge of, the occupier of the field or enclosure or the owner of the sheep or a person authorised by either of those persons ; or

(*b*) a police dog, a guide dog, a trained sheep dog, a working gun dog or a pack of hounds."

The Deer Act 1963

1963 c. 36.

4. For subsection (3) of section 10 of the Deer Act 1963 (general exceptions) there shall be substituted the following subsections—

" (3) A person shall not be guilty of an offence under section 3(1)(*c*)(i) of this Act by reason of the use of any smooth-bore gun for the purpose of killing any deer if he shows that the deer had been so seriously injured otherwise than by his unlawful act or was in such a condition that to kill it was an act of mercy.

(4) A person shall not be guilty of an offence under section 3(1)(*c*)(i) of this Act by reason of the use as a slaughtering instrument, for the purpose of killing any deer, of a smooth-bore gun which—

(*a*) is of not less gauge than 12 bore ;

(*b*) has a barrel less than 24 inches (609·6 millimetres) in length ; and

(*c*) is loaded with a cartridge purporting to contain shot none of which is less than ·203 inches (5·16 millimetres) in diameter (that is to say, size AAA or any larger size)."

5.—(1) After section 10 of that Act there shall be inserted the following section—

" Exceptions for authorised persons.

10A.—(1) Subject to subsection (3) of this section an authorised person shall not be guilty of an offence under section 1 of this Act by reason of—

(*a*) the taking or killing of any deer by means of shooting ; or

Sch. 7

(*b*) the injuring of any deer by means of shooting in an attempt to take or kill it,

on any cultivated land, pasture or enclosed woodland.

(2) Subject to subsection (3) of this section an authorised person shall not be guilty of an offence under section 3(1)(*c*)(i) of this Act by reason of the use, for the purpose of taking or killing any deer on any land, of any smooth-bore gun of not less gauge than 12 bore which is loaded with—

(*a*) a cartridge containing a single non-spherical projectile weighing not less than 350 grains (22·68 grammes) ; or

(*b*) a cartridge purporting to contain shot each of which is 203 inches (5·16 millimetres) in diameter (that is to say, size AAA).

(3) An authorised person shall not be entitled to rely on the defence provided by subsection (1) or (2) of this section as respects anything done in relation to any deer on any land unless he shows that—

(*a*) he had reasonable grounds for believing that deer of the same species were causing, or had caused, damage to crops, vegetables, fruit, growing timber or any other form of property on the land ;

(*b*) it was likely that further damage would be so caused and any such damage was likely to be serious ; and

(*c*) his action was necessary for the purpose of preventing any such damage.

(4) The Secretary of State and the agriculture Minister acting jointly may by order, either generally or in relation to any area or any species and description of deer specified in the order, repeal subsection (2) of this section or amend it by adding any firearm or ammunition or by altering the description of, or deleting, any firearm or ammunition mentioned in it, or by adding any further conditions which must be satisfied.

(5) Before making an order under subsection (4) of this section, the Secretary of State and the agriculture Minister shall consult organisations that appear to them to represent persons likely to be interested in or affected by the order.

(6) In this section—

'agriculture Minister' means the Minister of Agriculture, Fisheries and Food in relation to England and the Secretary of State for Wales in relation to Wales ;

'authorised person' means—

(*a*) the occupier of the land on which the action is taken ;

SCH. 7

(*b*) any member of the occupier's household normally resident on the occupier's land, acting with the written authority of the occupier;

(*c*) any person in the ordinary service of the occupier on the occupier's land, acting with the written authority of the occupier; or

(*d*) any person having the right to take or kill deer on the land on which the action is taken or any person acting with the written authority of a person having that right."

(2) In sections 1(1) and 3(1) of that Act for the words " sections 10 and 11 " there shall be substituted the words " sections 10, 10A and 11 ".

(3) For subsection (1) of section 12 of that Act (orders) there shall be substituted the following subsections—

" (1) Any power to make orders under this Act shall be exercisable by statutory instrument.

(1A) A statutory instrument containing an order under section 1(2) or 3(4) of this Act shall be subject to annulment in pursuance of a resolution of either House of Parliament.

(1B) No order under section 10A(4) of this Act shall be made unless a draft of the order has been laid before and approved by a resolution of each House of Parliament."

6.—(1) In paragraph 1 of Schedule 2 to that Act (prohibited firearms and ammunition) the words " of less gauge than 12 bore " shall be omitted.

(2) In paragraph 4 of that Schedule the words from " other than " onwards shall be omitted.

The Conservation of Seals Act 1970

1970 c. 30.

7.—(1) In subsection (1)(*c*) of section 10 of the Conservation of Seals Act 1970 (power to grant licences), the word " or " immediately following sub-paragraph (ii) shall be omitted and after sub-paragraph (iii) there shall be inserted the words " or

(iv) the protection of flora or fauna in an area to which subsection (4) of this section applies,".

(2) In subsection (3)(*b*) of that section for the words from " a nature reserve " onwards there shall be substituted the words " an area to which subsection (4) of this section applies ".

(3) After subsection (3) of that section there shall be inserted the following subsection—

" (4) This subsection applies to any area which—

(*a*) is a nature reserve within the meaning of section 15 of the National Parks and Access to the Countryside Act 1949;

(*b*) has been notified under section 28(1) of the Wildlife and Countryside Act 1981 (areas of special scientific interest);

SCH. 7

(*c*) is an area to which section 29(3) of that Act (special protection for certain areas of special scientific interest) applies ; or

(*d*) has been designated as a marine nature reserve under section 36 of that Act."

The Badgers Act 1973

8. For subsections (2) and (3) of section 1 of the Badgers Act 1973 (possession of recently killed badgers etc.) there shall be substituted the following subsections— 1973 c. 57.

"(2) If, save as permitted by or under this Act, any person has in his possession or under his control any dead badger or any part of, or anything derived from, a dead badger, he shall be guilty of an offence.

(3) A person shall not be guilty of an offence under subsection (2) above if he shows that—

(*a*) the badger had not been killed, or had been killed otherwise than in contravention of the provisions of this Act ; or

(*b*) the badger or other thing in his possession or control had been sold (whether to him or any other person) and, at the time of the purchase, the purchaser had had no reason to believe that the badger had been killed in contravention of those provisions."

9.—(1) Section 7 of that Act (exceptions for authorised persons) shall be omitted.

(2) In section 2(*c*) of that Act for the words "subject to section 7(3) of this Act" there shall be substituted the words "save as permitted by or under this Act".

(3) Section 6 of that Act (areas within which section 7(1) does not apply) shall be omitted.

(4) In subsection (2) of section 8 of that Act (general exceptions) paragraph (*c*) (live badger taken in circumstances in which, by virtue of section 7(1) or (2), the taking did not constitute an offence) shall be omitted.

(5) In section 11 of that Act (interpretation) the definitions of "area of special protection" and "authorised person" shall be omitted.

10.—(1) In section 8 of that Act (general exceptions), after subsection (1) there shall be inserted the following subsections—

"(1A) A person shall not be guilty of an offence under section 1(1) of this Act by reason of—

(*a*) the killing or taking or the attempted killing or taking of any badger, or

(*b*) the injuring of any badger in the course of taking it or attempting to kill or take it,

if he shows that his action was necessary for the purpose of preventing serious damage to land, crops, poultry or any other form of property.

SCH. 7

(1B) The defence provided by subsection (1A) above shall not apply in relation to any action taken at any time if it had become apparent, before that time, that that action would prove necessary for the purpose mentioned in that subsection and either—

(*a*) a licence under section 9 of this Act authorising that action had not been applied for as soon as reasonably practicable after that fact had become apparent ; or

(*b*) an application for such a licence had been determined ".

(2) In section 9 of that Act (licences) at the end of subsection (1) there shall be inserted the following paragraph—

" (*e*) for the purpose of preventing serious damage to land, crops, poultry or any other form of property, to kill or take badgers within an area specified in the licence by any means so specified."

(3) In subsection (2)(*b*) of that section after the words " paragraph (*d*) " there shall be inserted the words " or (*e*) ".

(4) After subsection (3) of that section there shall be inserted the following subsection—

" (4) The Minister of Agriculture, Fisheries and Food and the Secretary of State shall from time to time consult with the Nature Conservancy Council as to the exercise of their functions under subsection (1)(*e*) above ; and neither of them shall grant a licence of any description unless he has been advised by the Council as to the circumstances in which, in the Council's opinion, licences of that description should be granted."

11.—(1) In subsection (1)(*c*) of section 10 of that Act (enforcement, penalties etc.) for the words from " any badger " onwards there shall be substituted the words " anything which may be evidence of the commission of the offence or may be liable to be forfeited under subsection (3) below ".

(2) In subsection (2) of that section for " £20 " there shall be substituted " £200 " and for " £100 " there shall be substituted " £1,000 ".

12. In section 11 of that Act (interpretation) for the definition of " local authority " there shall be substituted the following definition—

" ' sale ' includes hire, barter and exchange and cognate expressions shall be construed accordingly."

Sections 13, 22 and 24.

SCHEDULE 8

PLANTS WHICH ARE PROTECTED

Common name	*Scientific name*
Alison, Small	Alyssum alyssoides
Broomrape, Bedstraw	Orobanche caryophyllacea
Broomrape, Oxtongue	Orobanche loricata

SCH. 8

Common name	*Scientific name*
Broomrape, Thistle	Orobanche reticulata
Calamint, Wood	Calamintha sylvatica
Catchfly, Alpine	Lychnis alpina
Cinquefoil, Rock	Potentilla rupestris
Club-rush, Triangular	Scirpus triquetrus
Cotoneaster, Wild	Cotoneaster integerrimus
Cow-wheat, Field	Melampyrum arvense
Cudweed, Jersey	Gnaphalium luteoalbum
Diapensia	Diapensia lapponica
Eryngo, Field	Eryngium campestre
Fern, Dickie's Bladder	Cystopteris dickieana
Fern, Killarney	Trichomanes speciosum
Galingale, Brown	Cyperus fuscus
Gentian, Alpine	Gentiana nivalis
Gentian, Spring	Gentiana verna
Germander, Water	Teucrium scordium
Gladiolus, Wild	Gladiolus illyricus
Hare's-ear, Sickle-leaved	Bupleurum falcatum
Hare's-ear, Small	Bupleurum baldense
Heath, Blue	Phyllodoce caerulea
Helleborine, Red	Cephalanthera rubra
Knawel, Perennial	Scleranthus perennis
Knotgrass, Sea	Polygonum maritimum
Lady's-slipper	Cypripedium calceolus
Lavender, Sea	Limonium paradoxum Limonium recurvum
Leek, Round-headed	Allium sphaerocephalon
Lettuce, Least	Lactuca saligna
Lily, Snowdon	Lloydia serotina
Marsh-mallow, Rough	Althaea hirsuta
Orchid, Early Spider	Ophrys sphegodes
Orchid, Fen	Liparis loeselii
Orchid, Ghost	Epipogium aphyllum
Orchid, Late Spider	Ophrys fuciflora
Orchid, Lizard	Himantoglossum hircinum
Orchid, Military	Orchis militaris
Orchid, Monkey	Orchis simia
Pear, Plymouth	Pyrus cordata
Pink, Cheddar	Dianthus gratianopolitanus
Pink, Childling	Petroraghia nanteuilii
Sandwort, Norwegian	Arenaria norvegica
Sandwort, Teesdale	Minuartia stricta
Saxifrage, Drooping	Saxifraga cernua
Saxifrage, Tufted	Saxifraga cespitosa
Solomon's-seal, Whorled	Polygonatum verticillatum
Sow-thistle, Alpine	Cicerbita alpina
Spearwort, Adder's-tongue	Ranunculus ophioglossifolius
Speedwell, Spiked	Veronica spicata
Spurge, Purple	Euphorbia peplis
Starfruit	Damasonium alisma
Violet, Fen	Viola persicifolia
Water-plantain, Ribbon leaved	Alisma gramineum
Wood-sedge, Starved	Carex depauperata

SCH. 8

Common name	*Scientific name*
Woodsia, Alpine	Woodsia alpina
Woodsia, Oblong	Woodsia ilvensis
Wormwood, Field	Artemisia campestris
Woundwort, Downy	Stachys germanica
Woundwort, Limestone	Stachys alpina
Yellow-rattle, Greater	Rhinanthus serotinus

NOTE. The common name or names given in the first column of this Schedule are included by way of guidance only; in the event of any dispute or proceedings, the common name or names shall not be taken into account.

Sections 14 and 22.

SCHEDULE 9

ANIMALS AND PLANTS TO WHICH SECTION 14 APPLIES

PART I

ANIMALS WHICH ARE ESTABLISHED IN THE WILD

Common name	*Scientific name*
Bass, Large-mouthed Black	Micropterus salmoides
Bass, Rock	Ambloplites rupestris
Bitterling	Rhodeus sericeus
Budgerigar	Melopsittacus undulatus
Capercaillie	Tetrao urogallus
Coypu	Myocastor coypus
Dormouse, Fat	Glis glis
Duck, Carolina Wood	Aix sponsa
Duck, Mandarin	Aix galericulata
Duck, Ruddy	Oxyura jamaicensis
Eagle, White-tailed	Haliaetus albicilla
Frog, Edible	Rana esculenta
Frog, European Tree (otherwise known as Common tree frog)	Hyla arborea
Frog, Marsh	Rana ridibunda
Gerbil, Mongolian	Meriones unguiculatus
Goose, Canada	Branta canadensis
Goose, Egyptian	Alopochen aegyptiacus
Heron, Night	Nycticorax nycticorax
Lizard, Common Wall	Podarcis muralis
Marmot, Prairie (otherwise known as Prairie dog)	Cynomys
Mink, American	Mustela vison
Newt, Alpine	Triturus alpestris
Parakeet, Ring-necked	Psittacula krameri
Partridge, Chukar	Alectoris chukar
Partridge, Rock	Alectoris graeca
Pheasant, Golden	Chrysolophus pictus
Pheasant, Lady Amherst's	Chrysolophus amherstiae
Pheasant, Reeves'	Syrmaticus reevesii
Pheasant, Silver	Lophura nycthemera
Porcupine, Crested	Hystrix cristata
Porcupine, Himalayan	Hystrix hodgsonii

SCH. 9

Common name	*Scientific name*
Pumpkinseed (otherwise known as Sun-fish or Pond-perch)	Lepomis gibbosus
Quail, Bobwhite	Colinus virginianus
Rat, Black	Rattus rattus
Squirrel, Grey	Sciurus carolinensis
Terrapin, European Pond	Emys orbicularis
Toad, African Clawed	Xenopus laevis
Toad, Midwife	Alytes obstetricans
Toad, Yellow-bellied	Bombina variegata
Wallaby, Red-necked	Macropus rufogriseus
Wels (otherwise known as European catfish)	Silurus glanis
Zander	Stizostedion lucioperca

PART II

PLANTS

Common name	*Scientific name*
Hogweed, Giant	Heracleum mantegazzianum
Kelp, Giant	Macrocystis pyrifera
Knotweed, Japanese	Polygonum cuspidatum
Seaweed, Japanese	Sargassum muticum

NOTE. The common name or names given in the first column of this Schedule are included by way of guidance only ; in the event of any dispute or proceedings, the common name or names shall not be taken into account.

SCHEDULE 10

Section 15.

AMENDMENTS OF THE ENDANGERED SPECIES (IMPORT AND EXPORT) ACT 1976

PART I

THE AMENDMENTS

Licences

1.—(1) After subsection (3) of section 1 of the 1976 Act (restriction on importation and exportation of certain animals and plants) there shall be inserted the following subsections—

" (3A) Subsection (3) above shall not apply in relation to an application of any description if the scientific authority concerned has advised the Secretary of State as to whether licences should be issued in pursuance of applications of that description and, if so, their terms.

(3B) Where the Secretary of State is satisfied that the issue of a licence authorising the importation or exportation of any item which—

(*a*) is part of or derives from or is made wholly or partly from an animal of any of the kinds to which Schedule 1 or a plant of any of the kinds to which Schedule 2 to this Act for the time being applies ; but

SCH. 10

(*b*) is not an item to which Schedule 3 to this Act for the time being applies,

would facilitate the importation or exportation of that item, he may, if he considers it expedient to do so, issue such a licence."

(2) In subsections (4), (5), (6) and (7) of that section after the words "subsection (2)" there shall be inserted the words "or (3B)".

(3) In subsection (4) of that section after paragraph (*a*) there shall be inserted the following paragraphs—

"(*aa*) may be issued either to all persons, to persons of a class or to a particular person;

(*ab*) may be subject to compliance with any specified conditions,";

and in paragraph (*c*) of that subsection for the words from "a period" to "shorter" there shall be substituted the word "such".

Expenses of returning animals and plants to the wild

2. After subsection (8) of section 1 of the 1976 Act there shall be inserted the following subsection—

"(9) Where, in the case of a live animal or plant of any kind which is condemned or deemed to be condemned as forfeited, the Commissioners of Customs and Excise incur any expenses in connection with, or with a view to—

(*a*) its return to the wild; or

(*b*) its being kept at premises (whether within or outside the United Kingdom) which are suitable for the keeping of animals or plants of that kind,

those expenses may be recovered, as a debt due to the Crown, from the importer or intending exporter of the animal or plant or any person possessing or having control of it at the time of its seizure.

In this subsection expressions which are also used in the Customs and Excise Management Act 1979 have the same meanings as in that Act."

Powers of entry

3. After the subsection inserted by paragraph 2 as subsection (9) of section 1 of the 1976 Act there shall be inserted the following subsections—

"(10) Any person duly authorised in writing by the Secretary of State may, at any reasonable time and (if required to do so) upon producing evidence that he is so authorised, enter any premises where animals of any of the kinds to which Schedule 1 or plants of any of the kinds to which Schedule 2 to this Act for the time being applies are kept (whether temporarily or permanently) in order to ascertain whether any of the animals or plants kept there have been imported contrary to this section.

(11) Any person who wilfully obstructs a person acting under subsection (10) above shall be liable on summary conviction to a fine not exceeding £200."

SCH. 10

Power to modify Schedules

4.—(1) In paragraph (*c*) of section 3 of the 1976 Act (power to modify Schedules) after the word " conservation " there shall be inserted the words " in any area " and after the word " endangered " there shall be inserted the word " there ".

(2) After paragraph (*d*) of that section there shall be inserted the following paragraph—

" (*dd*) to restrict the importation of animals or plants of any kind which appear to the Secretary of State to be unlikely to survive for any appreciable time if they are kept in the United Kingdom ;".

Sale of certain animals or plants or their derivatives

5.—(1) In subsection (1) of section 4 of the 1976 Act (offences to sell etc. things imported contrary to section 1 or their derivatives) for the words " Subject to subsection (2) " there shall be substituted the words " Subject to subsections (1B) and (2) ", after the words " has in his possession " there shall be inserted the words " or transports " and the words " and in the following provisions " onwards shall be omitted.

(2) After that subsection there shall be inserted the following subsections—

" (1A) Subject to subsections (1B) and (2) below, a person who sells, offers or exposes for sale, or has in his possession or transports for the purpose of sale—

(*a*) a live or dead animal of any of the kinds to which Schedule 4 to this Act for the time being applies or an egg or other immature stage of such an animal ;

(*b*) a live or dead plant of any of the kinds to which Schedule 5 to this Act for the time being applies ; or

(*c*) any part of or anything which derives from or is made wholly or partly from anything referred to in paragraph (*a*) or (*b*) above,

shall be guilty of an offence ; but nothing in this subsection shall apply in relation to anything falling within subsection (1) above or anything which has been imported, or is a part of or derives from or is made wholly or partly from anything which has been imported, before the passing of the Wildlife and Countryside Act 1981.

(1B) Subsections (1) and (1A) above do not apply to anything done under and in accordance with the terms of a licence issued by the Secretary of State ; and subsections (4) to (7) of section 1 above shall apply in relation to a licence issued under this subsection as they apply in relation to a licence issued under subsection (2) of that section.

(1C) In the following provisions of this section " restricted article " means anything falling within subsection (1) or (1A) above."

(3) In subsection (2) of that section after the words " subsection (1) " there shall be inserted the words " or (1A) ".

SCH. 10

(4) In subsection (5) of that section after the words " subsection (1) " there shall be inserted the words " , (1A) ".

(5) In subsection (6) of that section after the words "references to " there shall be inserted the word " hire ".

(6) After Schedule 3 to the 1976 Act there shall be inserted as Schedule 4 the Schedule set out in Part II of this Schedule.

(7) After the Schedule inserted in the 1976 Act by sub-paragraph (6) there shall be inserted as Schedule 5 the Schedule set out in Part III of this Schedule.

Supplemental

6. In section 13(2) of the 1976 Act (substitution in Northern Ireland of references to the Department of Agriculture for Northern Ireland for references to the Secretary of State in specified provisions) for the words " 1(2), (3) and (4), 2(4) " there shall be substituted the words " 1(2) to (4) and (10), 2(4), 4(1B) ".

PART II

SCHEDULE INSERTED AS SCHEDULE 4

SCHEDULE 4

ANIMALS THE SALE ETC. OF WHICH IS RESTRICTED

This Schedule applies to the following kinds of animal, namely—

MAMMALS

1. The kinds of mammal specified in the first column below—

Marsupials

Kind	*Common name*
Bettongia	Rat kangaroo
Caloprymnus campestris	Desert rat-kangaroo
Lagorchestes hirsutus	Western hare-wallaby
Lagostrophus fasciatus	Banded hare-wallaby
Onychogalea fraenata	Bridle nail-tailed wallaby
Onychogalea lunata	Crescent nail-tailed wallaby
Lasiorhinus krefftii	Queensland hairy-nosed wombat
Chaeropus ecaudatus	Pig-footed bandicoot
Macrotis lagotis	Rabbit-bandicoot
Macrotis leucura	Lesser rabbit-bandicoot
Perameles bougainville	Western barred bandicoot
Sminthopsis longicaudata	Long-tailed dunnart
Sminthopsis psammophila	Sandhill dunnart
Thylacinus cynocephalus	Tasmanian wolf

Primates

Allocebus	Hairy-eared dwarf lemur
Cheirogaleus	Dwarf lemurs
Hapalemur	Gentle lemurs
Lemur	Lemurs
Lepilemur	Sportive and weasel lemurs
Microcebus	Mouse lemurs
Phaner	Fork-marked mouse lemurs
Avahi	Avahis (otherwise known as Woolly indris)
Indri	Indris
Propithecus	Sifakas

SCH. 10

Kind	*Common name*
Daubentonia madagascariensis	Aye-aye
Callimico goeldii	Goeldi's marmoset (otherwise known as Goeldi's tamarin)
Callithrix aurita	White eared marmoset
Callithrix flaviceps	Buff-headed marmoset
Leontopithecus	Maned tamarin (otherwise known as Golden tamarin)
Saguinus bicolor	Pied tamarin
Saguinus geoffroyi	Geoffroy's tamarin
Saguinus leucopus	White-footed tamarin
Saguinus oedipus	Cotton-headed tamarin
Alouatta palliata (otherwise known as Alouatta villosa)	Mantled howler
Ateles geoffroyi frontatus	Black-browed spider monkey
Ateles geoffroyi panamensis	Red spider monkey
Brachyteles arachnoides	Woolly spider monkey
Cacajao	Uakaris
Chiropotes albinasus	White-nosed saki
Saimiri oerstedii	Red-backed squirrel monkey
Cercocebus galeritus galeritus	Tana River mangabey
Cercopithecus diana	Diana monkey
Colobus badius kirkii	Kirk's red colobus (otherwise known as Zanzibar red colobus)
Colobus badius rufomitratus	Tana River red colobus
Macaca silenus	Lion-tailed macaque
Nasalis larvatus	Proboscis monkey
Papio leucophaeus (otherwise known as Mandrillus leucophaeus)	Drill
Papio sphinx (otherwise known as Mandrillus sphinx)	Mandrill
Presbytis entellus	Langur (otherwise known as Entellus langur or True langur)
Presbytis geei	Golden langur
Presbytis pileatus	Caped langur
Presbytis potenziani	Mentawi leaf monkey
Pygathrix nemaeus	Douc langur
Rhinopithecus roxellanae	Snub-nosed langur
Simias concolor	Mentawi snub-nosed langur
Hylobates	Gibbons
Symphalangus syndactylus	Siamang
Pongidae	Great apes
Edentates	
Priodontes giganteus (otherwise known as Priodontes maximus)	Giant armadillo

SCH. 10

Pangolins

Kind	*Common name*
Manis temmincki	South African pangolin

Rabbits and hares

Caprolagus hispidus	Assam rabbit (otherwise known as Hispid hare)
Romerolagus diazi	Volcano rabbit

Rodents

Cynomys mexicanus	Mexican prairie marmot
Leporillus conditor	Australian sticknest rat
Pseudomys fumeus	Smoky mouse
Pseudomys praeconis	Shark Bay mouse
Xeromys myoides	False water rat
Zyzomys pendunculatus	Central thick-tailed rat
Chinchilla (except any domestic form of Chinchilla laniger)	Chinchilla

Cetaceans

Lipotes vexillifer	Chinese river dolphin
Physeter catodon (otherwise known as Physeter macrocephalus)	Sperm whale
Platanista gangetica	Ganges dolphin
Platanista minor	Indus river dolphin
Sotalia	Humpbacked dolphins
Sousa	Humpbacked dolphins
Neophocaena phocaenoides	Finless porpoise
Phocoena sinus	Cochito
Balaena mysticetus	Greenland right whale (otherwise known as Bowhead whale)
Balaenoptera borealis	Sei whale
Balaenoptera musculus	Blue whale
Balaenoptera physalus	Common rorqual
Eschrichtius	Grey whales
Eubalaena	Right whales
Megaptera novaeangliae	Humpback whale

Carnivores

Speothos venaticus	Bush dog
Vulpes velox hebes	Northern kit fox
Helarctos malayanus	Sun bear
Selenarctos thibetanus	Asiatic black bear
Tremarctos ornatus	Spectacled bear
Ursus arctos isabellinus	Brown bear
Ursus arctos nelsoni	Mexican brown bear
Ursus arctos pruinosus	Tibetan brown bear
Aonyx microdon	Cameroon clawless otter
Enhydra lutris nereis	Southern sea otter
Lutra felina	Marine otter
Lutra longicaudis	South American otter
Lutra lutra	Eurasian otter
Lutra provocax	Southern river otter

SCH. 10

Kind	*Common name*
Mustela nigripes	Black-footed ferret
Pteronura brasiliensis	Giant otter
Prionodon pardicolor	Spotted linsang
Hyaena brunnea	Brown hyaena
Acinonyx jubatus	Cheetah
Felis bengalensis bengalensis	Leopard cat
Felis concolor coryi	Florida puma
Felis concolor costaricensis	Costa Rica puma
Felis concolor cougar	Eastern puma
Felis jacobita	Andean cat
Felis rufa escuinapae	Mexican bobcat
Felis marmorata	Marbled cat
Felis nigripes	Black-footed cat
Felis pardalis mearnsi	Costa Rica ocelot
Felis pardalis mitis	Brazilian ocelot
Felis planiceps	Flat-headed cat
Felis rubiginosa	Rusty spotted cat
Felis temmincki	Asiatic golden cat
Felis tigrina oncilla	Little spotted cat
Felis wiedii nicaraguae	Nicaraguan margay
Felis wiedii salvinia	Guatemalan margay
Felis yagouaroundi cacomitli	Jaguarundi
Felis yagouaroundi fossata	Jaguarundi
Felis yagouaroundi panamensis	Jaguarundi
Felis yagouaroundi tolteca	Jaguarundi
Neofelis nebulosa	Clouded leopard
Panthera leo persica	Asiatic lion
Panthera onca	Jaguar
Panthera pardus	Leopard
Panthera tigris	Tiger
Panthera uncia	Snow leopard
Seals	
Arctocephalus townsendi	Guadelupe fur seal
Monachus	Monk seals
Elephants	
Elephas maximus	Asian elephant
Sea-cows	
Dugong dugon	Dugong (otherwise known as Sea-cow)
Trichechus inunguis	Amazonian manatee
Trichechus manatus	West Indian manatee
Odd-toed ungulates	
Equus grevyi	Grevy's zebra
Equus hemionus hemionus	Mongolian wild ass
Equus hemionus khur	Indian wild ass
Equus przewalskii	Przewalski's horse
Equus zebra zebra	Cape mountain zebra
Tapirus bairdii	Central American tapir
Tapirus indicus	Malayan tapir (otherwise known as Indian tapir)

SCH. 10

Kind	*Common name*
Tapirus pinchaque	Mountain tapir (otherwise known as Woolly tapir)
Rhinocerotidae	Rhinoceroses
	Even-toed ungulates
Babyrousa babyrussa	Babirusa
Sus salvanius	Pygmy hog
Vicugna vicugna	Vicugna
Axis calamianensis	Calamian deer
Axis kuhli	Bawean deer
Axis porcinus annamiticus	Thai hog deer
Blastocerus dichotomus	Marsh deer
Cervus duvauceli	Swamp deer
Cervus elaphus hanglu	Kashmir stag (otherwise known as Hanglu)
Cervus eldi	Brow-antlered deer
Dama mesopotamica	Persian fallow deer
Hippocamelus antisiensis	Peruvian huemal
Hippocamelus bisulcus	Chilean huemal
Moschus moschiferus moschiferus	Himalayan musk deer
Ozotoceros bezoarticus	Pampas deer
Pudu pudu	Chilean pudu
Antilocapra americana peninsularis	Lower California pronghorn
Antilocapra americana sonoriensis	Sonoran pronghorn
Bison bison athabascae	Wood bison
Bos gaurus	Gaur
Bos mutus	Wild yak
Bubalus depressicornis	Lowland anoa
Bubalus mindorensis	Tamaraw
Bubalus quarlesi	Mountain anoa
Capra falconeri chiltanensis	Markhor
Capra falconeri jerdoni	Markhor
Capra falconeri megaceros	Markhor
Capricornis sumatraensis	Serow
Hippotragus niger variani	Giant sable antelope
Nemorhaedus goral	Goral
Novibos sauveli	Koupray
Oryx leucoryx	Arabian oryx
Ovis ammon hodgsoni	Great Tibetan sheep
Ovis orientalis ophion	Cyprian mouflon
Ovis vignei	Urial
Pantholops hodgsoni	Tibetan antelope
Rupicapra rupicapra ornata	Abrussi chamois

BIRDS

2. The kinds of bird specified in the first column below—

	Rheas
Pterocnemia pennata	Lesser rhea
	Tinamous
Tinamus solitarius	Solitary tinamou

Kind	Common name
Penguins	
Spheniscus humboldti	Humboldt penguin
Grebes	
Podilymbus gigas	Atitlan grebe
Albatrosses	
Diomedea albatrus	Short-tailed albatross
Pelican-like birds	
Sula abbotti	Abbot's booby
Fregata andrewsi	Christmas Island frigatebird
Storks	
Ciconia ciconia boyciana	Japanese white stork
Geronticus eremita	Bald ibis
Nipponia nippon	Japanese crested ibis
Waterfowl	
Anas aucklandica nesiotis	Campbell Island Flightless teal
Anas laysanensis	Laysan duck
Anas oustaleti	Marianas Island duck (otherwise known as Marianas Mallard)
Branta canadensis leucopareia	Aleutian Canada goose
Branta sandvicensis	Hawaiian goose (otherwise known as Nene)
Cairina scutulata	White-winged wood duck
Rhodonessa caryophyllacea	Pink-headed duck
Diurnal Birds of Prey	
Cathartidae	New world vultures
Pandion haliaetus	Osprey
Accipitridae	True hawks
Sagittarius serpentarius	Secretary bird
Falconidae	Falcons
Gamebirds	
Aburria jacutinga	Black-fronted curassow (otherwise known as Black-fronted guan)
Aburria pipile	White-headed curassow (otherwise known as Piping guan)
Catreus wallichii	Cheer pheasant
Colinus virginianus ridgwayi	Masked bobwhite
Crax blumenbachii	Red-billed curassow
Crax mitu	Razor-billed curassow
Crossoptilon crossoptilon	White Eared-pheasant
Crossoptilon mantchuricum	Brown Eared-pheasant
Lophophorus impejanus	Himalayan monal
Lophophorus lhuysii	Chinese monal
Lophophorus sclateri	Sclater's monal
Lophura edwardsi	Edward's pheasant
Lophura imperialis	Imperial pheasant

SCH. 10

Kind	*Common name*
Lophura swinhoei	Swinhoe's pheasant
Macrocephalon maleo	Maleo Fowl
Oreophasis derbianus	Horned guan
Penelope albipennis	White-winged guan
Polyplectron emphanum	Palawan peacock pheasant
Syrmaticus ellioti	Elliot's pheasant
Syrmaticus humiae	Hume's pheasant (otherwise known as Bar-tailed pheasant)
Syrmaticus mikado	Mikado pheasant
Tetraogallus caspius	Caspian snowcock
Tetraogallus tibetanus	Tibetan snowcock
Tragopan blythii	Blyth's tragopan
Tragopan caboti	Cabot's tragopan
Tragopan melanocephalus	Western tragopan
Tympanuchus cupido attwateri	Attwater's prairie chicken
Cranes and rails	
Grus americana	Whooping crane
Grus canadensis nesiotes	Cuban sandhill crane
Grus canadensis pulla	Mississippi sandhill crane
Grus japonensis	Manchurian crane (otherwise known as Japanese crane)
Grus leucogeranus	Siberian White crane
Grus monacha	Hooded crane
Grus nigricollis	Black-necked crane
Grus vipio	White-necked crane (otherwise known as White-naped crane)
Tricholimnas sylvestris	Lord Howe wood-rail
Rhynochetos jubatus	Kagu
Chlamydotis undulata	Houbara bustard
Choriotis nigriceps (otherwise known as Ardeotis nigriceps)	Great Indian bustard
Eupodotis bengalensis	Bengal florican
Waders and Gulls	
Numenius borealis	Eskimo curlew
Tringa guttifer	Spotted greenshank (otherwise known as Nordmann's greenshank)
Larus relictus	Relict gull
Pigeons and doves	
Caloenas nicobarica	Nicobar pigeon
Ducula mindorensis	Mindoro imperial pigeon

Parrots

Kind	*Common name*
Amazona arausiaca	Red-necked parrot (otherwise known as Red-necked amazon)
Amazona barbadensis	Yellow-shouldered parrot (otherwise known as Yellow-shouldered amazon)
Amazona brasiliensis	Red-tailed parrot (otherwise known as Red-tailed amazon
Amazona guildingii	St. Vincent parrot (otherwise known as St. Vincent amazon)
Amazona imperialis	Imperial parrot (otherwise known as Imperial amazon)
Amazona leucocephala	Cuban parrot (otherwise known as Cuban amazon)
Amazona pretrei	Red-spectacled parrot (otherwise known as Red-spectacled amazon)
Amazona rhodocorytha (otherwise known as Amazona dufresniana rhodocorytha)	Red-crowned parrot (otherwise known as Red-crowned amazon)
Amazona versicolor	St Lucia parrot (otherwise known as St Lucia amazon)
Amazona vinacea	Vinaceous parrot (otherwise known as Vinaceous amazon)
Amazona vittata	Puerto Rico parrot (otherwise known as Puerto Rican amazon)
Anodorhynchus glaucus	Glaucous macaw
Anodorhynchus leari	Lear's macaw
Aratinga guaruba	Golden parakeet (otherwise known as Golden conure)
Cyanopsitta spixii	Spix's macaw
Cyanoramphus auriceps forbesi	Forbes' parakeet
Cyanoramphus novaezelandiae	Red-fronted parakeet
Cyclopsitta diophthalma coxeni (otherwise known as Opopsitta diophthalma coxeni)	Coxen's fig parrot
Geopsittacus occidentalis	Australian night parrot
Neophema chrysogaster	Orange-bellied parakeet (otherwise known as Orange-bellied parrot)
Pezoporus wallicus	Ground parrot

SCH. 10

Kind	*Common name*
Pionopsitta pileata	Red-capped parrot (otherwise known as Pileated parrot)
Psephotus chrysopterygius	Golden-shouldered parakeet (otherwise known as Golden-shouldered parrot or Hooded parakeet)
Psephotus pulcherrimus	Paradise parrot
Psittacula echo (otherwise known as Psittacula krameri echo)	Mauritius parakeet (otherwise known as Mauritius ring-necked parakeet)
Psittacus erithacus princeps	Fernando Po grey parrot
Pyrrhura cruentata	Blue-throated conure
Rhynchopsitta pachyrhyncha	Thick-billed parrot
Rhynchopsitta terrisi	Maroon-fronted parrot
Strigops habroptilus	Kakapo (otherwise known as Owl parrot)
	Hummingbirds
Ramphodon dohrnii	Hook-billed hermit
	Trogons
Pharomachrus mócinno costaricensis	Costa Rican quetzal (otherwise known as Resplendent quetzal)
Pharomachrus mocinno mocinno	Magnificent quetzal (otherwise known as Resplendent quetzal)
	Owls
Tytonidae	Barn owls
Strigidae	Typical owls
	Hornbills
Buceros bicornis (otherwise known as Buceros homrai)	Great pied hornbill
Rhinoplax vigil	Helmeted hornbill
	Woodpeckers
Campephilus imperialis	Imperial woodpecker
Dryocopus javensis richardsi	Tristram's woodpecker (otherwise known as White-bellied black woodpecker)
	Songbirds
Cotinga maculata	Banded cotinga
Xipholena atropurpurea	White-winged cotinga
Pitta kochi	Koch's pitta

SCH. 10

Kind	*Common name*
Atrichornis clamosa	Noisy scrub-bird
Leucopsar rothschildi	Rothschild's mynah
Dasyornis brachypterus longirostris	Western bristlebird
Dasyornis broadbenti littoralis	Western rufous bristlebird
Picathartes gymnocephalus	White-necked rockfowl (otherwise known as Yellow-headed rockfowl or Guinea bear-headed rockfowl)
Picathartes oreas	Grey-necked rockfowl (otherwise known as Cameroon bare-headed rockfowl or Red-headed rockfowl)
Zosterops albogularis	White-breasted silver-eye
Meliphaga cassidix	Helmeted honeyeater
Spinus cucullatus (otherwise known as Carduelis cucullatus)	Red siskin

REPTILES

3. The kinds of reptile specified in the first column below—

Crocodilians

Alligator sinensis	Chinese alligator
Caiman crocodilus apaporiensis	Rio Apaporis caiman (otherwise known as Spectacled caiman)
Caiman latirostris	Broad-nosed caiman
Melanosuchus niger	Black caiman
Crocodylus acutus	American crocodile
Crocodylus cataphractus	African slender-snouted crocodile (otherwise known as African sharp-nosed crocodile)
Crocodylus intermedius	Orinoco crocodile
Crocodylus moreletii	Morelet's crocodile
Crocodylus niloticus	Nile crocodile
Crocodylus novaeguineae mindorensis	Philippine crocodile
Crocodylus palustris	Mugger (otherwise known as Marsh crocodile or Broad-snouted crocodile)
Crocodylus porosus	Estuarine crocodile (otherwise known as Salt-water crocodile)
Crocodylus rhombifer	Cuban crocodile
Crocodylus siamensis	Siamese crocodile

SCH. 10

Kind	*Common name*
Osteolaemus tetraspis	West African dwarf crocodile
Tomistoma schlegelii	False gharial (otherwise known as False gavial)
Gavialis gangeticus	Indian gharial (otherwise known as Indian gavial)
Iguanas	
Brachylophus	Fijian iguanas
Cyclura	Caribbean rock iguanas
Sauromalus varius	San Esteban Island chuckwalla
Lizards	
Varanus bengalensis	Bengal monitor (otherwise known as Indian monitor or Common monitor)
Varanus flavescens	Yellow monitor
Varanus griseus	Desert monitor (otherwise known as Agra monitor or Grey monitor)
Varanus komodoensis	Komodo dragon
Snakes	
Acrantophis	Madagascar boas
Bolyeria	Round island boas
Casarea	Round island boas
Epicrates inornatus	Yellow tree boa
Epicrates subflavus	Jamaican boa
Python molurus molurus	Indian python (otherwise known as Indian rock python)
Sanzinia madagascariensis	Madagascar boa
Tuatara	
Sphenodon punctatus	Tuatara
Chelonians	
Batagur baska	River terrapin (otherwise known as Tuntong)
Geoclemys hamiltonii (otherwise known as Damonia hamiltonii)	Black pond turtle (otherwise known as Spotted pond turtle)
Melanochelys tricarinata (otherwise known as Geoemyda tricarinata or Nicoria tricarinata)	Three-keeled turtle (otherwise known as Three-keeled land tortoise)
Kachuga tecta tecta	Indian tent turtle (otherwise known as Indian sawback turtle or Roofed turtle or Dura turtle)

SCH. 10

Kind	*Common name*
Morenia ocellata	Burmese swamp turtle
Terrapene coahuila	Aquatic box turtle (otherwise known as Water box turtle)
Geochelone elephantopus (otherwise known as Testudo elephantopus)	Galapagos giant tortoise
Geochelone radiata (otherwise known as Testudo radiata)	Radiated tortoise (otherwise known as Rayed tortoise)
Geochelone yniphora (otherwise known as Testudo yniphora)	Madagascar tortoise (otherwise known as Rayed tortoise or Angonoka)
Gopherus flavomarginatus (otherwise known as Crophemus polyphemus flavomarginatus)	Mexican gopher tortoise
Psammobates geometricus (otherwise known as Testudo geometricus)	Geometric tortoise
Cheloniidae	Sea turtles
Dermochelys coriacea	Leatherback turtle (otherwise known as Leathery turtle or Luth)
Lissemys punctata punctata	Indian flap-shelled turtle
Trionyx ater	Cuatro Cienegas soft-shell turtle (otherwise known as Black soft-shelled turtle)
Trionyx gangeticus	Ganges soft-shelled turtle (otherwise known as Indian soft-shelled turtle)
Trionyx hurum	Peacock-marked soft-shelled turtle
Trionyx nigricans	Dark-coloured soft-shelled turtle
Pseudemydura umbrina	Short-necked turtle (otherwise known as Western swamp turtle)

AMPHIBIANS

4. The kinds of amphibian specified in the first column below—

Andrias davidianus (otherwise known as Megalobatrachus davidianus)	Chinese giant salamander
Andrias japonicus (otherwise known as Megalobatrachus japonicus)	Japanese giant salamander
Atelopus varius zeteki	Golden frog (otherwise known as Zetek's frog)
Bufo periglenes	Golden toad (otherwise known as Orange toad)
Bufo superciliaris	Cameroon toad
Nectophrynoides	Viviparous toads

SCH. 10

FISH

5. The kinds of fish specified in the first column below—

Kind	*Common name*
Acipenser brevirostrum	Shortnose sturgeon
Scleropages formosus	Asiatic bonytongue
Coregonus alpenae	Longjaw cisco
Chasmistes cujus	Cui-ui
Probarbus jullieni	Ikan temolek
Pangasianodon gigas	Giant catfish
Stizostedion vitreum glaucum	Blue walleye
Cynoscion macdonaldi	Drum fish

MOLLUSCS

6. The kinds of mollusc specified below—

Conradilla caelata
Dromus dromas
Epioblasma florentina curtisi (otherwise known as Dysnomia florentina curtisi)
Epioblasma florentina florentina (otherwise known as Dysnomia florentina florentina)
Epioblasma sampsoni (otherwise known as Dysnomia sampsoni)
Epioblasma sulcata perobliqua (otherwise known as Dysnomia sulcata perobliqua)
Epioblasma torulosa gubernaculum (otherwise known as Dysnomia torulosa gubernaculum)
Epioblasma torulosa torulosa (otherwise known as Dysnomia torulosa torulosa)
Epioblasma turgidula (otherwise known as Dysnomia turgidula)
Epioblasma walkeri (otherwise known as Dysnomia walkeri)
Fusconaia cuneolus
Fusconaia edgariana
Lampsilis higginsi
Lampsilis orbiculata orbiculata
Lampsilis satura
Lampsilis verescens
Plethobasus cicatricosus
Plethobasus cooperianus
Pleurobema plenum
Potamilus capax (otherwise known as Proptera capax)
Quadrula intermedia
Quadrula sparsa
Toxolasma cylindrella (otherwise known as Caruncululina cylindrella)
Unio nickliniana (otherwise known as Megalonaias nickliniana)
Unio tampicoensis tecomatensis (otherwise known as Lampsilis tampicoensis tecomatensis)
Villosa trabalis (otherwise known as Micromya trabalis)

NOTE. The second column of this Schedule gives a common name or names, where available, and is included by way of guidance only ; in the event of any dispute or proceedings, only the first column is to be taken into account.

PART III SCH. 10

SCHEDULE INSERTED AS SCHEDULE 5

SCHEDULE 5

PLANTS THE SALE ETC. OF WHICH IS RESTRICTED

This Schedule applies to the kinds of plant specified in the second column below—

Family	*Kind*
Apocynaceae	Pachypodium namaquanum
Araceae	Alocasia sanderana
Cactaceae	Ariocarpus agavoides
	Ariocarpus scapharostrus
	Aztekium ritteri
	Echinocereus lindsayi
	Obregonia denegrii
	Pelecyphora aselliformis
	Pelecyphora strobiliformis
Caryocaraceae	Caryocar costaricense
Caryophyllaceae	Gymnocarpus przewalskii
	Melandrium mongolicus
	Silene mongolica
	Stellaria pulvinata
Cupressaceae	Fitzroya cupressoides
	Pilgerodendron uviferum
Cycadaceae	Mirocycas calocoma
Gentianaceae	Prepusa hookeriana
Humiriaceae	Vantanea barbourii
Juglandaceae	Engelhardtia pterocarpa
Leguminosae	Ammopiptanthus mongolicum
	Cynometra hemitomophylla
	Platymiscium pleiostachyum
	Tachigalia versicolor
Liliaceae	Aloe albida
	Aloe pillansii
	Aloe polyphylla
	Aloe thorncropftii
	Aloe vossii
Melastomataceae	Lavoisiera itambana
Meliaceae	Guarea longipetiola
Moraceae	Batocarpus costaricensis
Nepenthaceae	Nepenthes rajah
Orchidaceae	Cattleya skinneri
	Cattleya trianae
	Didiciea cunninghamii
	Laelia jongheana
	Laelia lobata
	Lycaste virginalis var alba
	Peristeria elata
	Renanthera imschootiana
	Vanda coerulea

SCH. 10

Family—cont	*Kind*—cont.
Pinaceae	Abies guatemalensis
	Abies nebrodensis
Podocarpaceae	Podocarpus costalis
	Podocarpus parlatorei
Proteaceae	Orothamnus zeyheri
	Protea odorata
Rubiaceae	Balmea stormae
Sarraceniaceae	Sarracenia alabamensis alabamensis
	Sarracenia jonesii
	Sarracenia oreophila
Saxifragaceae (otherwise known as Grossulariaceae)	Ribes sardoum
Stangeriaceae	Stangeria eriopus
Ulmaceae	Celtis aetnensis
Welwitschiaceae	Welwitschia bainesii
Zamiaceae	Encephalartos
Zingiberaceae	Hedychium philippinense

Sections 29 and 34.

SCHEDULE 11

PROCEDURE IN CONNECTION WITH CERTAIN ORDERS UNDER PART II

Coming into operation

1.—(1) An original order or a restrictive amending order shall take effect on its being made.

(2) It shall be the duty of the Secretary of State to consider every original order or restrictive amending order made by him or a relevant authority, and any such order shall cease to have effect nine months after it is made unless the Secretary of State has previously given notice under paragraph 6 that he has considered it and does not propose to amend or revoke it or he has amended or revoked it or, in the case of an order made by such an authority, the authority has revoked it.

(3) An amending or revoking order, other than a restrictive amending order, made by a relevant authority shall be submitted by the authority to the Secretary of State for confirmation and shall not take effect until confirmed by him.

(4) Subject to paragraphs 3(1) and 4(4), an amending or revoking order, other than a restrictive amending order, made by the Secretary of State shall not take effect until confirmed by him.

(5) An amending or revoking order requiring confirmation shall, by virtue of this sub-paragraph, stand revoked if the Secretary of State gives notice under paragraph 6 that the order is not to be confirmed.

Publicity for orders

2.—(1) Where an order takes effect immediately, the authority making the order (whether the relevant authority or the Secretary of State) shall give notice—

(*a*) setting out the order or describing its general effect and in either case stating that it has taken effect;

(*b*) naming a place in the area in which the land to which the order relates is situated where a copy of the order may be inspected free of charge at all reasonable hours; and SCH. 11

(*c*) specifying the time (not being less than 28 days from the date of the first publication of the notice) within which, and the manner in which, representations or objections with respect to the order may be made.

(2) Where an order requires confirmation, the authority making the order shall give notice—

(*a*) setting out the order or describing its general effect and in either case stating that it has been made and requires confirmation; and

(*b*) stating in relation to it the matters specified in sub-paragraph (1)(*b*) and (*c*).

(3) Subject to sub-paragraph (4), the notice to be given under sub-paragraph (1) or (2) shall be given—

(*a*) by publication in the Gazette and also at least one local newspaper circulating in the area in which the land to which the order relates is situated;

(*b*) by serving a like notice on every owner and occupier of any of that land; and

(*c*) in the case of a notice given by the Secretary of State, by serving a like notice on the relevant authority in whose area the land to which the order relates is situated.

(4) The Secretary of State may, in any particular case, direct that it shall not be necessary to comply with sub-paragraph (3)(*b*); but if he so directs in the case of any land, then in addition to publication the notice shall be addressed to "The owners and any occupiers" of the land (describing it) and a copy or copies of the notice shall be affixed to some conspicuous object or objects on the land.

Unopposed orders

3.—(1) Where an order made by a relevant authority takes effect immediately and no representations or objections are duly made in respect of it or any so made are withdrawn,—

(*a*) the Secretary of State shall as soon as practicable after considering it decide either to take no action on the order or to make an order amending or revoking it (subject, however, to paragraph 5); and

(*b*) the amending or revoking order shall take effect immediately, but it shall not require confirmation and no representation or objection with respect to it shall be entertained.

(2) Where an order requiring confirmation is made and no representations or objections are duly made in respect of it or any so made are withdrawn, the Secretary of State may confirm the order (with or without modifications).

Opposed orders

4.—(1) If any representation or objection duly made with respect to an order is not withdrawn, then, as soon as practicable in the case of an order having immediate effect and before confirming an order requiring confirmation, the Secretary of State shall either—

(*a*) cause a local inquiry to be held; or

SCH 11

(*b*) afford any person by whom a representation or objection has been duly made and not withdrawn an opportunity of being heard by a person appointed by the Secretary of State for the purpose.

(2) On considering any representations or objections duly made and the report of any person appointed to hold the inquiry or to hear representations or objections, the Secretary of State—

(*a*) shall, if the order has already taken effect, decide either to take no action on the order or to make an order (subject, however, to paragraph 5) amending or revoking the order as the Secretary of State thinks appropriate in the light of the report, representations or objections, without consulting the relevant authority where that authority made the order ; or

(*b*) if the order requires confirmation, may confirm it (with or without modifications).

1972 c. 70.
1973 c. 65.

(3) The provisions of subsections (2) to (5) of section 250 of the Local Government Act 1972 or subsections (4) to (8) of section 210 of the Local Government (Scotland) Act 1973 (which relate to the giving of evidence at, and defraying the cost of, local inquiries) shall apply in relation to any inquiry held under this paragraph as they apply in relation to a local inquiry which a Minister causes to be held under subsection (1) of that section.

(4) An amending or revoking order made by virtue of this paragraph shall take effect immediately, but it shall not require confirmation and no representation or objection with respect to it shall be entertained.

Restriction on power to amend orders or confirm them with modifications

5. The Secretary of State shall not by virtue of paragraph 3(1) or 4(2) amend an order which has taken effect, or confirm any other order with modifications, so as to extend the area to which an original order applies.

Notice of final decision on orders

6.—(1) The Secretary of State shall as soon as practicable after making an order by virtue of paragraph 3(1) or 4(2) give notice—

(*a*) setting out the order or describing its general effect and in either case stating that it has taken effect ; and

(*b*) stating the name of the place in the area in which the land to which the order relates is situated where a copy of the order may be inspected free of charge at all reasonable hours.

(2) The Secretary of State shall give notice of any of the following decisions of his as soon as practicable after making the decision—

(*a*) a decision under paragraph 3(1) or 4(2) to take no action on an order which has already taken effect ;

(*b*) a decision to confirm or not to confirm an order requiring confirmation under this Schedule.

(3) A notice under this paragraph of a decision to confirm an order shall— Sch. 11

(*a*) set out the order as confirmed or describe its general effect, and in either case state the day on which the order took effect;

(*b*) state the name of the place in the area in which the land to which the order relates is situated where a copy of the order as confirmed may be inspected free of charge at all reasonable hours.

(4) A notice under this paragraph shall be given by publishing it in accordance with paragraph 2(3) and serving a copy of it on any person on whom a notice was required to be served under paragraph 2(3) or (4).

Proceedings for questioning validity of orders

7.—(1) This paragraph applies to any order which has taken effect and as to which the Secretary of State has given notice under paragraph 6 of a decision of his to take no action or to amend the order in accordance with paragraph 3 or 4; and in this paragraph " the relevant notice " means any such notice.

(2) If any person is aggrieved by an order to which this paragraph applies and desires to question its validity on the ground that it is not within the powers of section 29 or 34, as the case may be, or that any of the requirements of this Schedule have not been complied with in relation to it, he may within six weeks from the date of the relevant notice make an application to the Court under this paragraph.

(3) On any such application the Court may, if satisfied that the order is not within those powers or that the interests of the applicant have been substantially prejudiced by a failure to comply with any of those requirements—

(*a*) in England and Wales, quash the order, or any provision of the order, either generally or in so far as it affects the interests of the applicant; or

(*b*) in Scotland, make such declarator as seems to the Court to be appropriate.

(4) Except as provided by this paragraph, the validity of an order shall not be questioned in any legal proceedings whatsoever.

(5) In this paragraph " the Court " means the High Court in relation to England and Wales and the Court of Session in relation to Scotland.

Interpretation

8. In this Schedule—

" amending order " and " revoking order " mean an order which amends or, as the case may be, revokes a previous order;

" the Gazette " means—

(*a*) if the order relates in whole or in part to England and Wales, the London Gazette;

SCH. 11

(*b*) if the order relates in whole or in part to Scotland, the Edinburgh Gazette ;

" order " means an order under section 29 or 34 ;

" original order " means an order other than an amending or revoking order ;

" the relevant authority " has the same meaning as in section 34 ;

" restrictive amending order " means an amending order which extends the area to which a previous order applies.

Section 36.

SCHEDULE 12

PROCEDURE IN CONNECTION WITH ORDERS UNDER SECTION 36

Consultation

1. Before making an order, the Secretary of State shall consult with such persons as he may consider appropriate.

Publicity for draft orders

2.—(1) Before making an order, the Secretary of State shall prepare a draft of the order and give notice—

(*a*) stating that he proposes to make the order and the general effect of it ;

(*b*) naming a place in the area in which the land to which the draft order relates is situated where a copy of the draft order, and of any byelaws made or proposed to be made by a relevant authority for the protection of the area specified in the draft order, may be inspected free of charge, and copies thereof may be obtained at a reasonable charge, at all reasonable hours ; and

(*c*) specifying the time (not being less than 28 days from the date of the first publication of the notice) within which, and the manner in which, representations or objections with respect to the draft order may be made.

(2) Subject to sub-paragraph (3), the notice to be given under sub-paragraph (1) shall be given—

(*a*) by publication in the Gazette and also at least one local newspaper circulating in the area in which the land to which the draft order relates is situated ;

(*b*) by serving a like notice on—

(i) every person in whom is vested an interest in or right over any of that land ;

(ii) every relevant authority whose area includes any of that land ; and

(iii) such other bodies as may be prescribed or as the Secretary of State may consider appropriate ; and

(*c*) by causing a copy of the notice to be displayed in a prominent position—

(i) at council offices in the locality of the land to which the draft order relates ; and

(ii) at such other places as the Secretary of State may consider appropriate. SCH. 12

(3) The Secretary of State may, in any particular case, direct that it shall not be necessary to comply with sub-paragraph (2)(*b*)(i).

(4) Subject to sub-paragraph (3), sub-paragraph (2)(*b*) and (*c*) shall be complied with not less than 28 days before the expiration of the time specified in the notice.

Unopposed orders

3. If no representations or objections are duly made, or if any so made are withdrawn, the Secretary of State may make the order with or without modifications.

Opposed orders

4.—(1) If any representation or objection duly made is not withdrawn the Secretary of State shall, before making the order, either—

(*a*) cause a local inquiry to be held ; or

(*b*) afford any person by whom a representation or objection has been duly made and not withdrawn an opportunity of being heard by a person appointed by the Secretary of State for the purpose.

(2) On considering any representations or objections duly made and the report of the person appointed to hold the inquiry or hear representations or objections, the Secretary of State may make the order with or without modifications.

Restriction on power to make orders with modifications

5.—(1) The Secretary of State shall not make an order with modifications so as—

(*a*) to affect land not affected by the draft order ; or

(*b*) to authorise the making of any byelaw not authorised by the draft order,

except after complying with the requirements of sub-paragraph (2).

(2) The said requirements are that the Secretary of State shall—

(*a*) give such notice as appears to him requisite of his proposal so to modify the order, specifying the time (which shall not be less than 28 days from the date of the first publication of the notice) within which, and the manner in which, representations or objections with respect to the proposal may be made ;

(*b*) hold a local inquiry or afford any person by whom any representation or objection has been duly made and not withdrawn an opportunity of being heard by a person appointed by the Secretary of State for the purpose ; and

(*c*) consider the report of the person appointed to hold the inquiry or to hear representations or objections.

Local inquiries

6.—(1) The provisions of subsections (2) to (5) of section 250 of the Local Government Act 1972 or subsections (4) to (8) of section 210 1972 c. 70.

SCH. 12 of the Local Government (Scotland) Act 1973 (which relate to the giving of evidence at, and defraying the cost of, local inquiries) shall apply in relation to any inquiry held under paragraph 4 or 5 as they apply in relation to a local inquiry which a Minister causes to be held under subsection (1) of that section.

1973 c. 65.

(2) A local inquiry caused to be held under paragraph 4 or 5 before the making of an order may be held concurrently with any local inquiry caused to be held before the confirmation of byelaws made by a relevant authority for the protection of the area specified in the order.

Notice of making of orders

7.—(1) As soon as practicable after an order is made, the Secretary of State shall give notice—

(*a*) describing the general effect of the order as made and stating the date on which it took effect ; and

(*b*) naming a place in the area in which the land to which the order relates is situated where a copy of the order as made may be inspected free of charge, and copies thereof may be obtained at a reasonable charge, at all reasonable hours.

(2) A notice under sub-paragraph (1) shall be given—

(*a*) by publication in the manner required by paragraph 2(2)(*a*) ;

(*b*) by serving a like notice on any persons on whom notices were required to be served under paragraph 2(2)(*b*) ; and

(*c*) by causing like notices to be displayed in the like manner as the notices required to be displayed under paragraph 2(2)(*c*).

Proceedings for questioning validity of orders

8.—(1) If any person is aggrieved by an order which has taken effect and desires to question its validity on the ground that it is not within the powers of section 36 or that any of the requirements of this Schedule have not been complied with in relation to it, he may within 42 days from the date of publication of the notice under paragraph 7 make an application to the Court under this paragraph.

(2) On any such application the Court may, if satisfied that the order is not within those powers or that the interests of the applicant have been substantially prejudiced by a failure to comply with those requirements—

(*a*) in England and Wales, quash the order, or any provision of the order, either generally or in so far as it affects the interests of the applicant ; or

(*b*) in Scotland, make such declarator as seems to the Court to be appropriate.

(3) Except as provided by this paragraph, the validity of an order shall not be questioned in any legal proceedings whatever.

(4) In this paragraph " the Court " means the High Court in relation to England and Wales and the Court of Session in relation to Scotland.

Supplemental

Sch. 12

9.—(1) In this Schedule—

"area" includes district;

"council offices" means offices or buildings acquired or provided by a local authority;

"the Gazette" means—

(*a*) if the order relates in whole or in part to England and Wales, the London Gazette;

(*b*) if the order relates in whole or in part to Scotland, the Edinburgh Gazette;

"order" means an order under section 36;

"prescribed" means prescribed by regulations made by the Secretary of State;

and expressions to which a meaning is assigned by section 36 have the same meanings in this Schedule as in that section.

(2) References in this Schedule to land include references to any waters covering it; and for the purposes of this Schedule any area in Great Britain which is bounded by tidal waters or parts of the sea shall be taken to include—

(*a*) the waters adjacent to that area up to the seaward limits of territorial waters; and

(*b*) the land covered by the said adjacent waters.

(3) Regulations under this Schedule shall be made by statutory instrument which shall be subject to annulment in pursuance of a resolution of either House of Parliament.

SCHEDULE 13

Section 47.

PROVISIONS WITH RESPECT TO THE COUNTRYSIDE COMMISSION

Status

1. The Commission shall be a body corporate.

2. The Commission shall not be regarded as the servant or agent of the Crown, or as enjoying any status, immunity or privilege of the Crown; and the Commission's property shall not be regarded as property of, or property held on behalf of, the Crown.

Members

3.—(1) The Commission shall consist of a chairman and such number of other members as the Secretary of State may determine, of whom one may be appointed to be deputy chairman.

(2) The members of the Commission shall be appointed by the Secretary of State and shall hold and vacate office in accordance with such terms as may be prescribed by or under regulations made by the Secretary of State and, on vacating office, shall be eligible for re-appointment.

SCH. 13

(3) Regulations under sub-paragraph (2) shall be made by statutory instrument which shall be subject to annulment in pursuance of a resolution of either House of Parliament.

(4) A member may at any time by notice in writing to the Secretary of State resign his office.

4.—(1) The Commission—

(*a*) shall pay to their members such remuneration and allowances (if any) as the Secretary of State may, with the approval of the Minister, determine ; and

(*b*) as regards any member in whose case the Secretary of State may, with the approval of the Minister, so determine, shall pay such pension to or in respect of him, or make such payments towards the provision of such pension as the Secretary of State may, with the Minister's approval, determine.

(2) If a person ceases to be a member of the Commission, and it appears to the Secretary of State that there are special circumstances which make it right that he should receive compensation, the Secretary of State may, with the approval of the Minister, require the Commission to pay to that person a sum of such amount as the Secretary of State may, with the Minister's approval, determine.

Committee for Wales

5.—(1) The Commission shall, after consultation with the Secretary of State, appoint a Committee for Wales.

(2) The membership of the Committee for Wales shall consist partly of persons who are members of the Commission, one of whom shall be the chairman of the Committee, and partly of persons, not exceeding such number as the Secretary of State may for the time being approve, who are not members of the Commission.

(3) The Commission may, after consulting the Secretary of State and subject to such conditions as they think appropriate, delegate any of their functions in Wales to the Committee for Wales, including (for Wales) their advisory functions under section 2 of the 1968 Act, and their duty of making recommendations under that section in respect of local authorities' applications for Exchequer grants.

(4) The Commission may, in the case of such members of the Committee for Wales as are not members of the Commission, pay to them such reasonable allowances in respect of—

(*a*) expenses properly incurred in the performance of their duties ;

(*b*) loss of remunerative time ; or

(*c*) additional expenses (other than as aforesaid) necessarily incurred by them for the purpose of enabling them to perform their duties, being expenses to which they would not otherwise have been subject,

as the Secretary of State may, with the approval of the Minister, determine.

Procedure

6. The procedure (including the quorum) of the Commission shall be such as they may determine.

7. The validity of any proceeding of the Commission shall not be affected by any vacancy among the members thereof or by any defect in the appointment of a member thereof. SCH. 13

Staff

8.—(1) The Commission shall appoint—

(*a*) with the approval of the Secretary of State, a chief officer and

(*b*) such number of other employees as they may with the approval of the Secretary of State and the Minister determine.

(2) The Commission shall pay to their employees such remuneration and allowances as they may with the approval of the Secretary of State and the Minister determine.

(3) In the case of any person to be employed by them on and after the appointed day who immediately before that day was a civil servant, the Commission shall ensure that, so long as he is engaged in duties reasonably comparable to those in which he was engaged immediately before the coming into force of this Schedule, the terms and conditions of his employment, taken as a whole, are not less favourable than those which he then enjoyed.

(4) In relation to any person who—

(*a*) is a civil servant before the appointed day ; and

(*b*) is as from that day employed by the Commission,

Schedule 13 to the Employment Protection (Consolidation) Act 1978 (ascertainment, for the purposes of that Act and section 119 of the Employment Protection Act 1975, of the length of an employee's period of employment and whether that employment has been continuous) shall have effect as if his service as a civil servant had been employment under the Commission. 1978 c. 44. 1975 c. 71.

9.—(1) The Commission shall in the case of such of their employees as they may with the approval of the Secretary of State and the Minister determine,—

(*a*) pay such pension to or in respect of them ;

(*b*) make such payments towards the provision of such pensions ; or

(*c*) provide and maintain such schemes (whether contributory or not) for the payment of such pensions,

as they may with the approval of the Secretary of State and the Minister determine.

(2) In this paragraph any reference to the payment of pensions to or in respect of the Commission's employees includes a reference to the payment of pensions by way of compensation to or in respect of any of the Commission's employees who suffer loss of office or employment or loss or diminution of emoluments.

10.—(1) Employment with the Commission shall be included among the kinds of employment to which a superannuation scheme under section 1 of the Superannuation Act 1972 can apply, and 1972 c. 11.

Sch. 13

accordingly in Schedule 1 to that Act (in which those kinds of employment are listed) the words " Countryside Commission " shall be inserted after the words " Monopolies Commission ".

(2) The Commission shall pay to the Minister at such times in each financial year as may be determined by the Minister, subject to any directions of the Treasury, sums of such amounts as he may so determine for the purposes of this paragraph as being equivalent to the increase during the year of such liabilities of his under the Principal Civil Service Pension Scheme as are attributable to the provision of pensions to or in respect of persons who are, or have been, in the service of the Commission in so far as that increase results from the service of those persons during that financial year and to the expense to be incurred in administering those pensions.

Accounts and report

11.—(1) The Commission shall keep proper accounts and other records, and shall prepare for each financial year a statement of account in such form as the Secretary of State with the approval of the Treasury may direct and submit those statements of account to the Secretary of State at such time as he may with the approval of the Treasury direct.

(2) The Secretary of State shall, as respects each financial year, send the Commission's statement of accounts to the Comptroller and Auditor General not later than the end of November following the year.

(3) The Comptroller and Auditor General shall examine, certify and report on the statement of accounts and lay copies of it, together with his report, before each House of Parliament.

12. The Commission shall furnish the Secretary of State with such returns, accounts and other information with respect to their property and activities or proposed activities as he may from time to time require, and shall afford to the Secretary of State facilities for the verification of information so furnished and for that purpose permit any person authorised in that behalf by the Secretary of State to inspect and make copies of the Commission's accounts, books, documents or papers and give that person such explanation of them as he may reasonably require.

13.—(1) The Commission shall, as soon as possible after the end of each financial year, make to the Secretary of State a report on the discharge by them of their functions under the 1949 Act, the 1968 Act and this Act during that year.

(2) Without prejudice to the generality of sub-paragraph (1), but subject to the provisions of sub-paragraph (3), the report of the Commission for any year shall include—

(*a*) a statement of the action taken by the Commission to promote the enjoyment of the countryside by members of the public who are disabled ; and (*b*) a record of all questions with which the Commission have been concerned during that year and which appear to the Commission to be of general public interest, indicating the purport of any representations or recommendations made by the Commission with respect thereto, and the conclusions (if any) reached thereon. SCH. 13

(3) The report of the Commission for any year shall set out any direction given by the Secretary of State during that year under section 3 of the 1949 Act unless the Secretary of State has notified to the Commission his opinion that it is against the interests of national security so to do.

(4) The Secretary of State shall lay a copy of every report of the Commission under this paragraph before each House of Parliament.

Land

14. The Commission, for the purpose of providing themselves with office or other accommodation in connection with the exercise of any of their functions, may, with the approval of the Secretary of State, acquire land, erect and maintain buildings or other structures thereon, and, when the land is no longer required for such purpose, dispose of it.

15. Any land occupied by the Commission shall, for the purpose of any rate on property, be treated as if it were property occupied by or on behalf of the Crown for public purposes.

Interpretation

16. In this Schedule—

" appointed day " means the day appointed for the coming into force of this Schedule ;

" the Commission " means the Countryside Commission ;

" financial year " means the period commencing with the appointed day and ending with 31st March following that day, and each successive period of twelve months ;

" the Minister " means the Minister for the Civil Service ;

" pension " includes allowance or gratuity.

SCHEDULE 14

Section 53.

APPLICATIONS FOR CERTAIN ORDERS UNDER PART III

Form of applications

1. An application shall be made in the prescribed form and shall be accompanied by—

(*a*) a map drawn to the prescribed scale and showing the way or ways to which the application relates ; and

(*b*) copies of any documentary evidence (including statements of witnesses) which the applicant wishes to adduce in support of the application.

SCH. 14

Notice of applications

2.—(1) Subject to sub-paragraph (2), the applicant shall serve a notice stating that the application has been made on every owner and occupier of any land to which the application relates.

(2) If, after reasonable inquiry has been made, the authority are satisfied that it is not practicable to ascertain the name or address of an owner or occupier of any land to which the application relates, the authority may direct that the notice required to be served on him by sub-paragraph (1) may be served by addressing it to him by the description " owner " or " occupier " of the land (describing it) and by affixing it to some conspicuous object or objects on the land.

(3) When the requirements of this paragraph have been complied with, the applicant shall certify that fact to the authority.

(4) Every notice or certificate under this paragraph shall be in the prescribed form.

Determination by authority

3.—(1) As soon as reasonably practicable after receiving a certificate under paragraph 2(3), the authority shall—

(*a*) investigate the matters stated in the application ; and

(*b*) after consulting with every local authority whose area includes the land to which the application relates, decide whether to make or not to make the order to which the application relates.

(2) If the authority have not determined the application within twelve months of their receiving a certificate under paragraph 2(3), then, on the applicant making representations to the Secretary of State, the Secretary of State may, after consulting with the authority, direct the authority to determine the application before the expiration of such period as may be specified in the direction.

(3) As soon as practicable after determining the application, the authority shall give notice of their decision by serving a copy of it on the applicant and any person on whom notice of the application was required to be served under paragraph 2(1).

Appeal against a decision not to make an order

4.—(1) Where the authority decide not to make an order, the applicant may, at any time within 28 days after service on him of notice of the decision, serve notice of appeal against that decision on the Secretary of State and the authority.

(2) If on considering the appeal the Secretary of State considers that an order should be made, he shall give to the authority such directions as appear to him necessary for the purpose.

Interpretation

5.—(1) In this Schedule—

" application " means an application under section 53(5) ;

"local authority" means a district council, the Greater London Council, a parish or community council or the parish meeting of a parish not having a separate parish council; Sch. 14

"prescribed" means prescribed by regulations made by the Secretary of State.

(2) Regulations under this Schedule shall be made by statutory instrument which shall be subject to annulment in pursuance of a resolution of either House of Parliament.

SCHEDULE 15

Sections 53 and 54.

Procedure in Connection with Certain Orders Under Part III

Consultation

1. Before making an order, the authority shall consult with every local authority whose area includes the land to which the order relates.

Coming into operation

2. An order shall not take effect until confirmed either by the authority or the Secretary of State under paragraph 6 or by the Secretary of State under paragraph 7.

Publicity for orders

3.—(1) On making an order, the authority shall give notice in the prescribed form—

(*a*) describing the general effect of the order and stating that it has been made and requires confirmation;

(*b*) naming a place in the area in which the land to which the order relates is situated where a copy of the order may be inspected free of charge, and copies thereof may be obtained at a reasonable charge, at all reasonable hours; and

(*c*) specifying the time (not being less than 42 days from the date of the first publication of the notice) within which, and the manner in which, representations or objections with respect to the order may be made.

(2) Subject to sub-paragraph (4), the notice to be given under sub-paragraph (1) shall be given—

(*a*) by publication in at least one local newspaper circulating in the area in which the land to which the order relates is situated;

(*b*) by serving a like notice on—

(i) every owner and occupier of any of that land;

(ii) every local authority whose area includes any of that land;

(iii) every person on whom notice is required to be served in pursuance of sub-paragraph (3); and

(iv) such other persons as may be prescribed in relation to the area in which that land is situated or as the authority may consider appropriate; and

SCH. 15

(*c*) by causing a copy of the notice to be displayed in a prominent position—

(i) at the ends of so much of any way as is affected by the order;

(ii) at council offices in the locality of the land to which the order relates; and

(iii) at such other places as the authority may consider appropriate.

(3) Any person may, on payment of such reasonable charge as the authority may consider appropriate, require an authority to give him notice of all such orders as are made by the authority during a specified period, are of a specified description and relate to land comprised in a specified area; and in this sub-paragraph "specified" means specified in the requirement.

(4) The Secretary of State may, in any particular case, direct that it shall not be necessary to comply with sub-paragraph (2)(*b*)(i); but if he so directs in the case of any land, then in addition to publication the notice shall be addressed to "The owners and any occupiers" of the land (describing it) and a copy or copies of the notice shall be affixed to some conspicuous object or objects on the land.

(5) Sub-paragraph (2)(*b*) and (*c*) and, where applicable, sub-paragraph (4) shall be complied with not less than 42 days before the expiration of the time specified in the notice.

(6) A notice required to be served by sub-paragraph (2)(*b*) on the owner or occupier of any land, or on a local authority, shall be accompanied by a copy of so much of the order as relates to that land or, as the case may be, the area of that authority; and a notice required to be served by that sub-paragraph on such other persons as may be prescribed or as the authority may consider appropriate shall be accompanied by a copy of the order.

(7) A notice required to be displayed by sub-paragraph (2)(*c*) at the ends of so much of any way as is affected by the order shall be accompanied by a plan showing the general effect of the order so far as it relates to that way.

(8) At any time after the publication of a notice under this paragraph and before the expiration of the period specified in the notice for the making of representations and objections, any person may require the authority to inform him what documents (if any) were taken into account in preparing the order and—

(*a*) as respects any such documents in the possession of the authority, to permit him to inspect them and take copies; and

(*b*) as respects any such documents not in their possession, to give him any information the authority have as to where the documents can be inspected;

and on any requirement being made under this sub-paragraph the authority shall comply therewith within 14 days of the making of the requirement.

(9) Nothing in sub-paragraph (8) shall be construed as limiting the documentary or other evidence which may be adduced at any local inquiry or hearing held under paragraph 7 or 8. SCH. 15

Representations or objections made with respect to abandoned surveys or reviews

4.—(1) This paragraph applies where a survey begun under sections 27 to 32 of the 1949 Act, or a review begun under section 33 of that Act, is abandoned after a draft map and statement have been prepared.

(2) If an order modifies the definitive map and statement so as—

(*a*) to show any particulars shown in the draft map and statement but not in the definitive map and statement ; or

(*b*) to omit any particulars shown in the definitive map and statement but not in the draft map and statement,

any representation or objection duly made with respect to the showing in or omission from the draft map and statement of those particulars shall be treated for the purposes of paragraphs 6 and 7 as a representation or objection duly made with respect to the corresponding modifications made by the order.

Severance of orders

5.—(1) Where at any time representations or objections duly made and not withdrawn relate to some but not all of the modifications made by an order, the authority may, by notice given to the Secretary of State, elect that, for the purposes of the following provisions of this Schedule, the order shall have effect as two separate orders—

(*a*) the one comprising the modifications to which the representations or objections relate ; and

(*b*) the other comprising the remaining modifications.

(2) Any reference in sub-paragraph (1) to an order includes a reference to any part of an order which, by virtue of one or more previous elections under that sub-paragraph, has effect as a separate order.

Unopposed orders

6.—(1) If no representations or objections are duly made, or if any so made are withdrawn, the authority may—

(*a*) confirm the order without modification ; or

(*b*) if they require any modification to be made, submit the order to the Secretary of State for confirmation by him.

(2) Where an order is submitted to the Secretary of State under sub-paragraph (1), the Secretary of State may confirm the order with or without modifications.

Opposed orders

7.—(1) If any representation or objection duly made is not withdrawn the authority shall submit the order to the Secretary of State for confirmation by him.

SCH. 15

(2) Where an order is submitted to the Secretary of State under sub-paragraph (1), the Secretary of State shall either—

(*a*) cause a local inquiry to be held ; or

(*b*) afford any person by whom a representation or objection has been duly made and not withdrawn an opportunity of being heard by a person appointed by the Secretary of State for the purpose.

(3) On considering any representations or objections duly made and the report of the person appointed to hold the inquiry or hear representations or objections, the Secretary of State may confirm the order with or without modifications.

Restriction on power to confirm orders with modifications

8.—(1) The Secretary of State shall not confirm an order with modifications so as—

(*a*) to affect land not affected by the order ;

(*b*) not to show any way shown in the order or to show any way not so shown ; or

(*c*) to show as a highway of one description a way which is shown in the order as a highway of another description,

except after complying with the requirements of sub-paragraph (2).

(2) The said requirements are that the Secretary of State shall—

(*a*) give such notice as appears to him requisite of his proposal so to modify the order, specifying the time (which shall not be less than 28 days from the date of the first publication of the notice) within which, and the manner in which, representations or objections with respect to the proposal may be made ;

(*b*) hold a local inquiry or afford any person by whom any representation or objection has been duly made and not withdrawn an opportunity of being heard by a person appointed by the Secretary of State for the purpose ; and

(*c*) consider the report of the person appointed to hold the inquiry or to hear representations or objections.

Local inquiries

9.—The provisions of subsections (2) to (5) of section 250 of the
1972 c. 70. Local Government Act 1972 (which relate to the giving of evidence at, and defraying the cost of, local inquiries) shall apply in relation to any inquiry held under paragraph 7 or 8 as they apply in relation to a local inquiry which a Minister causes to be held under subsection (1) of that section.

Appointment of inspectors etc.

10.—(1) A decision of the Secretary of State under paragraph 6, 7 or 8 shall, except in such classes of case as may for the time being be prescribed or as may be specified in directions given by the Secretary of State, be made by a person appointed by the Secretary of State for the purpose instead of by the Secretary of State ; and a decision made by a person so appointed shall be treated as a decision of the Secretary of State.

(2) The Secretary of State may, if he thinks fit, direct that a decision which, by virtue of sub-paragraph (1) and apart from this sub-paragraph, falls to be made by a person appointed by the Secretary of State shall instead be made by the Secretary of State ; and a direction under this sub-paragraph shall state the reasons for which it is given and shall be served on the person, if any, so appointed, the authority and any person by whom a representation or objection has been duly made and not withdrawn. SCH. 15

(3) Where the Secretary of State has appointed a person to make a decision under paragraph 6, 7 or 8 the Secretary of State may, at any time before the making of the decision, appoint another person to make it instead of the person first appointed to make it.

(4) Where by virtue of sub-paragraph (2) or (3) a particular decision falls to be made by the Secretary of State or any other person instead of the person first appointed to make it, anything done by or in relation to the latter shall be treated as having been done by or in relation to the former.

(5) Regulations under this paragraph may provide for the giving of publicity to any directions given by the Secretary of State under this paragraph.

Notice of final decisions on orders

11.—(1) As soon as practicable after a decision to confirm an order is made or, in the case of a decision by the Secretary of State, as soon as practicable after receiving notice of his decision, the authority shall give notice—

(*a*) describing the general effect of the order as confirmed and stating that it has been confirmed (with or without modification) and the date on which it took effect ; and

(*b*) naming a place in the area in which the land to which the order relates is situated where a copy of the order as confirmed may be inspected free of charge, and copies thereof may be obtained at a reasonable charge, at all reasonable hours.

(2) A notice under sub-paragraph (1) shall be given—

(*a*) by publication in the manner required by paragraph 3(2)(*a*);

(*b*) by serving a like notice on any persons on whom notices were required to be served under paragraph 3(2)(*b*) or (4) ; and

(*c*) by causing like notices to be displayed in the like manner as the notices required to be displayed under paragraph 3(2)(*c*).

(3) A notice required to be served by sub-paragraph (2)(*b*) on the owner or occupier of any land, or on a local authority, shall be accompanied by a copy of so much of the order as confirmed as relates to that land or, as the case may be, the area of that authority ;

SCH. 15

and, in the case of an order which has been confirmed with modifications, a notice required to be served by that sub-paragraph on such other persons as may be prescribed or as the authority may consider appropriate shall be accompanied by a copy of the order as confirmed.

(4) As soon as practicable after a decision not to confirm an order or, in the case of a decision by the Secretary of State, as soon as practicable after receiving notice of his decision, the authority shall give notice of the decision by serving a copy of it on any persons on whom notices were required to be served under paragraph 3(2)(*b*) or (4).

Proceedings for questioning validity of orders

12.—(1) If any person is aggrieved by an order which has taken effect and desires to question its validity on the ground that it is not within the powers of section 53 or 54 or that any of the requirements of this Schedule have not been complied with in relation to it, he may within 42 days from the date of publication of the notice under paragraph 11 make an application to the High Court under this paragraph.

(2) On any such application the High Court may, if satisfied that the order is not within those powers or that the interests of the applicant have been substantially prejudiced by a failure to comply with those requirements, quash the order, or any provision of the order, either generally or in so far as it affects the interests of the applicant.

(3) Except as provided by this paragraph, the validity of an order shall not be questioned in any legal proceedings whatsoever.

Supplemental

13.—(1) The Secretary of State may, subject to the provisions of this Schedule, by regulations make such provision as to the procedure on the making, submission and confirmation of orders as appears to him to be expedient.

(2) In this Schedule—

"council offices" means offices or buildings acquired or provided by the authority or by a local authority;

"local authority" means a district council, the Greater London Council, a parish or community council or the parish meeting of a parish not having a separate parish council;

"order" means an order to which the provisions of this Schedule apply;

"prescribed" means prescribed by regulations made by the Secretary of State.

(3) Regulations under this Schedule shall be made by statutory instrument which shall be subject to annulment in pursuance of a resolution of either House of Parliament.

SCHEDULE 16

Section 63.

ORDERS CREATING, EXTINGUISHING OR DIVERTING FOOTPATHS OR BRIDLEWAYS

The Town and Country Planning Act 1971

1.—(1) In sub-paragraph (1)(*b*) of paragraph 1 of Schedule 20 to the Town and Country Planning Act 1971 (procedure in connection with orders relating to footpaths and bridleways) after the word "charge" there shall be inserted the words "and copies thereof may be obtained at a reasonable charge". 1971 c. 78.

(2) In sub-paragraph (2) of that paragraph—

(*a*) in head (*a*) the words "in the London Gazette and" shall be omitted;

(*b*) at the end of head (*b*) there shall be inserted the words—

"(iv) every person on whom notice is required to be served in pursuance of sub-paragraph (2A) of this paragraph; and

(v) such other persons as may be prescribed in relation to the area in which that land is situated or as the authority may consider appropriate; and"; and

(*c*) for head (*c*) there shall be substituted the following head—

"(*c*) by causing a copy of the notice to be displayed in a prominent position—

(i) at the ends of so much of any footpath or bridleway as is to be stopped up, diverted or extinguished by the order;

(ii) at council offices in the locality of the land to which the order relates; and

(iii) at such other places as the authority may consider appropriate".

(3) After that sub-paragraph there shall be inserted the following sub-paragraph—

"(2A) Any person may, on payment of such reasonable charge as the authority may consider appropriate, require an authority to give him notice of all such orders under section 210 or 214(1)(*b*) of this Act as are made by the authority during a specified period, are of a specified description and relate to land comprised in a specified area; and in this sub-paragraph 'specified' means specified in the requirement."

(4) At the end of sub-paragraph (3) of that paragraph there shall be inserted the words "and 'council offices' means offices or buildings acquired or provided by a council or by the council of a parish or community or the parish meeting of a parish not having a separate parish council".

(5) After sub-paragraph (4) of that paragraph there shall be inserted the following sub-paragraphs—

"(5) Sub-paragraph (2)(*b*) and (*c*) and, where applicable, sub-paragraph (4) of this paragraph shall be complied with not less than 28 days before the expiration of the time specified in the notice.

SCH. 16

(6) A notice required to be served by sub-paragraph (2)(*b*)(i), (ii), (iii) or (v) of this paragraph shall be accompanied by a copy of the order.

(7) A notice required to be displayed by sub-paragraph (2)(*c*)(i) of this paragraph at the ends of so much of any way as is affected by the order shall be accompanied by a plan showing the general effect of the order so far as it relates to that way."

2. After paragraph 3 of that Schedule there shall be inserted the following paragraph—

"3A.—(1) A decision of the Secretary of State under paragraph 3 of this Schedule shall, except in such classes of case as may for the time being be prescribed or as may be specified in directions given by the Secretary of State, be made by a person appointed by the Secretary of State for the purpose instead of by the Secretary of State; and a decision made by a person so appointed shall be treated as a decision of the Secretary of State.

(2) The Secretary of State may, if he thinks fit, direct that a decision which, by virtue of sub-paragraph (1) of this paragraph and apart from this sub-paragraph, falls to be made by a person appointed by the Secretary of State shall instead be made by the Secretary of State; and a direction under this sub-paragraph shall state the reasons for which it is given and shall be served on the person, if any, so appointed, the authority and any person by whom a representation or objection has been duly made and not withdrawn.

(3) Where the Secretary of State has appointed a person to make a decision under paragraph 3 of this Schedule the Secretary of State may, at any time before the making of the decision, appoint another person to make it instead of the person first appointed to make it.

(4) Where by virtue of sub-paragraph (2) or (3) of this paragraph a particular decision falls to be made by the Secretary of State or any other person instead of the person first appointed to make it, anything done by or in relation to the latter shall be treated as having been done by or in relation to the former.

(5) Regulations under this Act may provide for the giving of publicity to any directions given by the Secretary of State under this paragraph."

3.—(1) In paragraph 6 of that Schedule—

(*a*) for the words "a copy thereof" there shall be substituted the words "a copy of the order";

(*b*) after the words "free of charge" there shall be inserted the words "and copies thereof may be obtained at a reasonable charge"; and

(*c*) for heads (*a*) and (*b*) there shall be substituted the following heads—

"(*a*) serve a like notice on any persons on whom notices were required to be served under paragraph 1(2)(*b*) or (4) of this Schedule; and (*b*) cause like notices to be displayed in the like manner as the notices required to be displayed under paragraph 1(2)(*c*) of this Schedule: ". SCH. 16

(2) That paragraph as so amended shall be renumbered as paragraph 6(1) of that Schedule and after that provision as so renumbered there shall be inserted the following sub-paragraphs—

" (2) A notice required to be served by sub-paragraph (1)(*a*) of this paragraph on—

(*a*) a person on whom notice was required to be served by paragraph 1(2)(*b*)(i), (ii) or (iii) of this Schedule; or

(*b*) in the case of an order which has been confirmed with modifications, a person on whom notice was required to be served by paragraph 1(2)(*b*)(v) of this Schedule,

shall be accompanied by a copy of the order as confirmed.

(3) As soon as may be after a decision not to confirm an order under the said section 210 or 214(1)(*b*), the authority by whom the order was made shall give notice of the decision by serving a copy of it on any persons on whom notices were required to be served under paragraph 1(2)(*b*) or (4) of this Schedule. "

4. After that paragraph there shall be inserted the following paragraph—

" 7. As soon as may be after an order under section 210 or 214(1)(*b*) of this Act has come into operation otherwise than—

(*a*) on the date on which it was confirmed by the Secretary of State or confirmed as an unopposed order; or

(*b*) at the expiration of a specified period beginning with that date,

the authority by whom the order was made shall give notice of its coming into operation by publication in at least one local newspaper circulating in the area in which the land to which the order relates is situated.".

The Highways Act 1980

5.—(1) In subsection (1) of section 119 of the Highways Act 1980 (diversion of footpaths and bridleways) for the words from the beginning to " or on to land " there shall be substituted the words " Where it appears to a council as respects a footpath or bridleway in their area (other than one that is a trunk road or a special road) that, in the interests of the owner, lessee or occupier of land crossed by the path or way or of the public, it is expedient that the line of the path or way, or part of that line, should be diverted (whether on to land of the same or ". 1980 c. 66.

SCH. 16

(2) In subsection (5) of that section for the words " the council may require the owner, lessee or occupier on whose representations they are acting " there shall be substituted the words " on the representations of an owner, lessee or occupier of land crossed by the path or way, the council may require him ".

6.—(1) In sub-paragraphs (1)(*b*) and 2(*b*) of paragraph 1 of Schedule 6 to that Act (procedure as to certain orders relating to footpaths and bridleways) after the words " free of charge " there shall be inserted the words " and copies thereof may be obtained at a reasonable charge ".

(2) For sub-paragraph (3) of that paragraph there shall be substituted the following sub-paragraph—

" (3) The notices to be given under sub-paragraph (1) or (2) above shall be given—

(*a*) by publication in at least one local newspaper circulating in the area in which the land to which the order relates is situated;

(*b*) by serving a like notice on—

(i) every owner, occupier and lessee (except tenants for a month or any period less than a month and statutory tenants within the meaning of the Rent (Agriculture) Act 1976 or the Rent Act 1977) of any of that land;

(ii) every council, the council of every parish or community and the parish meeting of every parish not having a separate parish council, being a council, parish or community whose area includes any of that land;

(iii) every person on whom notice is required to be served in pursuance of sub-paragraph (3A) or (3B) below; and

(iv) such other persons as may be prescribed in relation to the area in which that land is situated or as the authority or, as the case may be, the Secretary of State may consider appropriate; and

(*c*) by causing a copy of the notice to be displayed in a prominent position—

(i) at the ends of so much of any footpath or bridleway as is created, stopped up or diverted by the order;

(ii) at council offices in the locality of the land to which the order relates; and

(iii) at such other places as the authority or, as the case may be, the Secretary of State may consider appropriate."

(3) After that sub-paragraph there shall be inserted the following sub-paragraphs— SCH. 16

"(3A) Any person may, on payment of such reasonable charge as the authority may consider appropriate, require an authority to give him notice of all such public path creation orders, public path extinguishment orders and public path diversion orders as are made by the authority during a specified period, are of a specified description and relate to land comprised in a specified area; and in this sub-paragraph "specified" means specified in the requirement.

(3B) Any person may, on payment of such reasonable charge as the Secretary of State may consider appropriate, require the Secretary of State to give him notice of all such draft public path creation orders, draft public path extinguishment orders and draft public path diversion orders as are prepared by the Secretary of State during a specified period, are of a specified description and relate to land comprised in a specified area; and in this sub-paragraph "specified" means specified in the requirement.

(3C) The Secretary of State may, in any particular case, direct that it shall not be necessary to comply with sub-paragraph (3)(*b*)(i) above; but if he so directs in the case of any land, then in addition to publication the notice shall be addressed to 'The owners and any occupiers' of the land (describing it) and a copy or copies of the notice shall be affixed to some conspicuous object or objects on the land."

(4) After sub-paragraph (4) of that paragraph there shall be inserted the following sub-paragraphs—

"(4A) Sub-paragraph (3)(*b*) and (*c*) and, where applicable, sub-paragraphs (3C) and (4) above shall be complied with not less than 28 days before the expiration of the time specified in the notice.

(4B) A notice required to be served by sub-paragraph (3)(*b*)(i), (ii) or (iv) above shall be accompanied by a copy of the order.

(4C) A notice required to be displayed by sub-paragraph (3)(*c*)(i) above at the ends of so much of any way as is affected by the order shall be accompanied by a plan showing the general effect of the order so far as it relates to that way.

(4D) In sub-paragraph (3)(*c*)(ii) above 'council offices' means offices or buildings acquired or provided by a council or by the council of a parish or community or the parish meeting of a parish not having a separate parish council."

7. After paragraph 2 of that Schedule there shall be inserted the following paragraph—

"2A—(1) A decision of the Secretary of State under paragraph 2 above as respects an order made by an authority other than the Secretary of State shall, except in such classes of case as may for the time being be prescribed or as may be specified in

SCH. 16

directions given by the Secretary of State, be made by a person appointed by the Secretary of State for the purpose instead of by the Secretary of State; and a decision made by a person so appointed shall be treated as a decision of the Secretary of State.

(2) The Secretary of State may, if he thinks fit, direct that a decision which, by virtue of sub-paragraph (1) above and apart from this sub-paragraph, falls to be made by a person appointed by the Secretary of State shall instead be made by the Secretary of State; and a direction under this sub-paragraph shall state the reasons for which it is given and shall be served on the person, if any, so appointed, the authority and any person by whom a representation or objection has been duly made and not withdrawn.

(3) Where the Secretary of State has appointed a person to make a decision under paragraph 2 above the Secretary of State may, at any time before the making of the decision, appoint another person to make it instead of the person first appointed to make it.

(4) Where by virtue of sub-paragraph (2) or (3) above a particular decision falls to be made by the Secretary of State or any other person instead of the person first appointed to make it, anything done by or in relation to the latter shall be treated as having been done by or in relation to the former.

(5) Provision may be made by regulations of the Secretary of State for the giving of publicity to any directions given by the Secretary of State under this paragraph."

8.—(1) In paragraph 4 of that Schedule after the words "free of charge" there shall be inserted the words "and copies thereof may be obtained at a reasonable charge" and for heads (*a*) and (*b*) there shall be substituted the following heads—

"(*a*) serve a like notice on any persons on whom notices were required to be served under paragraph 1(3)(*b*), (3C) or (4) above; and

(*b*) cause like notices to be displayed in the like manner as the notices caused to be displayed under paragraph 1(3)(*c*) above;".

(2) That paragraph as so amended shall be renumbered as paragraph 4(1) of that Schedule and after that provision as so renumbered there shall be inserted the following sub-paragraphs—

"(2) A notice required to be served by sub-paragraph (1)(*a*) above, on—

(*a*) a person on whom notice was required to be served by paragraph 1(3)(*b*)(i) or (ii) above; or

(*b*) in the case of an order which has been confirmed or made with modifications, a person on whom notice was required to be served by paragraph 1(3)(*b*)(iv) above,

shall be accompanied by a copy of the order as confirmed or made.

(3) As soon as may be after a decision not to confirm an order to which this Schedule applies, the authority by whom the order was made shall give notice of the decision by serving a copy of it on any persons on whom notices were required to be served under paragraph 1(3)(*b*), (3C) or (4) above.". Sch. 16

9. After that paragraph there shall be inserted the following paragraph—

"4A. As soon as may be after an order to which this Schedule applies has come into operation otherwise than—

(*a*) on the date on which it was confirmed or made by the Secretary of State or confirmed as an unopposed order; or

(*b*) at the expiration of a specified period beginning with that date,

the authority by whom the order was made or, in the case of an order made by the Secretary of State, the Secretary of State shall give notice of its coming into operation by publication in at least one local newspaper circulating in the area in which the land to which the order relates is situated."

Supplemental

10.—(1) The amendments made by the foregoing provisions of this Schedule shall not apply in relation to any order if it was made or a draft thereof was prepared, or a notice relating to it was given under paragraph 1 of the relevant Schedule, before the commencement date.

(2) Any reference in this paragraph to Schedule 6 to the Highways Act 1980 includes a reference to that Schedule as applied by paragraph 3 of the provisions of Part I of Schedule 3 to the 1968 Act which relate to the Acquisition of Land (Authorisation Procedure) Act 1946. 1980 c. 66. 1946 c. 49.

SCHEDULE 17

Section 73.

Enactments Repealed

Part I

Enactments repealed one month after the passing of this Act

Chapter	Short title	Extent of repeal
12, 13 & 14 Geo. 6. c. 97.	The National Parks and Access to the Countryside Act 1949.	Section 23.
1968 c. 41.	The Countryside Act 1968.	Section 14. In section 15(1) the words "which is not for the time being managed as a nature reserve but".

SCH. 17

Chapter	Short title	Extent of repeal
1973 c. 37.	The Water Act 1973.	In section 22(3) the words " not being land for the time being managed as a nature reserve".
1973 c. 54.	The Nature Conservancy Council Act 1973.	Section 3.
1973 c. 65.	The Local Government (Scotland) Act 1973.	In Schedule 27, in Part II, paragraph 101.
1980 c. 66.	The Highways Act 1980.	In section 134, subsection (3) and in subsection (5) the words " (3) or ". In section 135(1), the words " 6 or " and " 6 weeks or ".

PART II

ENACTMENTS REPEALED ON A DAY TO BE APPOINTED

Chapter	Short title	Extent of repeal
2 & 3 Geo. 5 c. 14.	The Protection of Animals (Scotland) Act 1912.	In section 9 the words " or any snare " and " or snare ".
12, 13 & 14 Geo. 6. c. 97.	The National Parks and Access to the Countryside Act 1949.	Sections 2 and 4. Sections 27 to 35. Section 38. Section 95.
2 & 3 Eliz. 2. c. 30.	The Protection of Birds Act 1954.	The whole Act.
1963 c. 33.	The London Government Act 1963.	In section 60, subsections (1) to (4).
1963 c. 36.	The Deer Act 1963.	In Schedule 2, in paragraph 1 the words " of less gauge than 12 bore " and in paragraph 4 the words from " other than " onwards.
1964 c. 59.	The Protection of Birds Act 1954 (Amendment) Act 1964.	The whole Act.
1967 c. 46.	The Protection of Birds Act 1967.	The whole Act.
1968 c. 41.	The Countryside Act 1968.	In section 1, subsection (4) and, in subsection (5), the words " and 2(1) " and the words " and in section 4(1) " onwards. Section 3. In Schedule 3, in Part I, the entry relating to the National Parks and Access to the Countryside Act 1949, and Parts II, III and IV.

SCH. 17

Chapter	Short title	Extent of repeal
1970 c. 30.	The Conservation of Seals Act 1970.	In section 10(1)(*c*), the word " or " immediately following sub-paragraph (ii).
1971 c. 23.	The Courts Act 1971.	In Schedule 8, paragraph 31. In Schedule 9, in Part II, the entry relating to section 31 of the National Parks and Access to the Countryside Act 1949.
1971 c. 78.	The Town and Country Planning Act 1971.	In Schedule 20, in paragraph 1(2)(*a*), the words " in the London Gazette and ".
1972 c. 70.	The Local Government Act 1972.	In Schedule 17, paragraphs 22 to 33. In Schedule 29, paragraph 37.
1973 c. 37.	The Water Act 1973.	In Schedule 8, paragraph 67.
1973 c. 54.	The Nature Conservancy Council Act 1973.	In section 5(3) the words from the beginning to " save as aforesaid ". In Schedule 1, paragraphs 3, 5, 7 and 12(*a*) and (*c*).
1973 c. 57.	The Badgers Act 1973.	Sections 6 and 7. Section 8(2)(*c*). In section 11, the definitions of " area of special protection " and " authorised person ".
1973 c. 65.	The Local Government (Scotland) Act 1973.	In Schedule 27, in Part II, paragraphs 115 and 168.
1975 c. 21.	The Criminal Procedure (Scotland) Act 1975.	In Schedule 7C, the entries relating to the Protection of Birds Act 1954 and the Conservation of Wild Creatures and Wild Plants Act 1975.
1975 c. 48.	The Conservation of Wild Creatures and Wild Plants Act 1975.	The whole Act.
1976 c. 16.	The Statute Law (Repeals) Act 1976.	In Schedule 2, in Part II, the entry relating to the Protection of Birds Act 1967.
1976 c. 72.	The Endangered Species (Import and Export) Act 1976.	Section 13(6).
1977 c. 45.	The Criminal Law Act 1977.	In Schedule 6, the entries relating to the Protection of Birds Act 1954 and the Conservation of Wild Creatures and Wild Plants Act 1975.
1979 c. 2.	The Customs and Excise Management Act 1979.	In Schedule 4, in paragraph 12, in the Table the entry relating to the Protection of Birds Act 1954.
1980 c. 66.	The Highways Act 1980.	In section 31(10) the words " or of that subsection " onwards. Section 340(2)(*d*).
1981 c. 22.	The Animal Health Act 1981.	In Schedule 5, paragraph 1

SCH. 17

Chapter	Short title	Extent of repeal
1981 c. 37.	The Zoo Licensing Act 1981.	In section 4(5), the entries relating to the Protection of Birds Acts 1954 to 1967 and the Conservation of Wild Creatures and Wild Plants Act 1975.

PRODUCED IN THE UK FOR W.J. SHARP
Controller and Chief Executive of Her Majesty's Stationery Office
and Queen's Printer of Acts of Parliament
LONDON: PUBLISHED BY HER MAJESTY'S STATIONERY OFFICE

PS 5353381 Dd.905469 C20 8/85 CCP